D1557218

RATIONALISM, PLATONISM AND GOD

PROCEEDINGS OF THE BRITISH ACADEMY • 149

RATIONALISM, PLATONISM AND GOD

Edited by
MICHAEL AYERS

Published for THE BRITISH ACADEMY
by OXFORD UNIVERSITY PRESS

Oxford University Press, Great Clarendon Street, Oxford OX2 6DP

Oxford New York
Auckland Cape Town Dar es Salaam Hong Kong Karachi
Kuala Lumpur Madrid Melbourne Mexico City Nairobi
New Delhi Shanghai Taipei Toronto

With offices in
Argentina Austria Brazil Chile Czech Republic France Greece
Guatemala Hungary Italy Japan Poland Portugal Singapore
South Korea Switzerland Thailand Turkey Ukraine Vietnam

Published in the United States
by Oxford University Press Inc., New York

© *The British Academy 2007*

Database right The British Academy (maker)

First published 2007

British Library Cataloguing in Publication Data
Data available

Library of Congress Cataloging in Publication Data
Data available

Typeset by Intype Libra Ltd, London
Printed in Great Britain
on acid-free paper by

Antony Rowe Ltd,
Chippenham, Wiltshire

ISBN 978–0–19–726420–1

ISSN 0068–1202

Contents

Contents

Notes on Contributors

Robert Merrihew Adams is a Senior Research Fellow in Philosophy at Mansfield College, Oxford. He taught philosophy for 35 years at the University of Michigan, UCLA, and Yale University. He has published extensively on metaphysics, ethics, the philosophy of religion, and the history of modern philosophy, and is the author of *Leibniz: Determinist, Theist, Idealist* (1994). He is a Fellow of the American Academy of Arts and Sciences and of the British Academy.

Maria Rosa Antognazza is Reader in the Philosophy of Religion at King's College London. She works on early modern philosophy, with a specific interest in religious epistemology, philosophical theology, and the theological and philosophical foundations of religious toleration. Her publications include *Leibniz on the Trinity and the Incarnation: Reason and Revelation in the Seventeenth Century* (Yale University Press, 2007) and *Leibniz: An Intellectual Biography* (Cambridge University Press, in press).

Michael Ayers was Professor of Philosophy at the University of Oxford until his retirement in 2002, and is Emeritus Fellow of Wadham College, Oxford. He is a Fellow of the British Academy. His publications on the history of philosophy have for the most centred on early modern empiricism (including, in 1991, *Locke*, a two-volume work on Locke's *Essay concerning Human Understanding*). More recently he has written on Descartes and on the origins of modern idealism. Since the sixties he has argued, and tried to show, that a historical or contexualist approach to the historiography of philosophy is in general philosophically more rewarding than the then common practice among analytical philosophers of attempting to identify and assess philosophical content in abstraction from historical circumstances.

John Cottingham is currently Professor of Philosophy at the University of Reading, where he holds an Established Chair of Philosophy, and is also Honorary Fellow of St John's College, Oxford. In 2002–2004 he was Stanton Lecturer in the Philosophy of Religion at Cambridge University. His most recent books are *Philosophy and the Good Life: reason and the passions in Greek, Cartesian and psychoanalytic ethics* (Cambridge, 1998), *On the Meaning of Life* (Routledge, 2003), and *The Spiritual Dimension* (Cambridge, 2005). His numerous other publications include *Descartes* (Blackwell, 1996), *The Rationalists* (Oxford University Press, 1988), and (as co-translator and editor) *The Philosophical Writings of Descartes* (Cambridge, 1985–91). His *Western Philosophy: an anthology* (Blackwell, 1996) is shortly to be re-issued in an augmented second edition; and he is general editor of the Oxford Philosophical Texts series. He is (since 1993) editor of *RATIO*, the international journal of analytic philosophy.

Douglas Hedley teaches the Philosophy of Religion in the Faculty of Divinity at the University of Cambridge and is a Fellow of Clare College. His interests revolve around contemporary philosophical theology and the history of Platonism. He was educated at the universities of Oxford and Munich. He is a past President of the European Society for the Philosophy of Religion; he was Directeur d'études invité at the EPHE, Sorbonne, Paris, and has held the Alan Richardson lectureship at Durham University. He gave the Teape lectures in India in 2006. Dr Hedley has co-edited with Sarah Hutton *Platonism at the Origins of Modernity* (Springer, 2007) and has published extensively on the Cambridge Platonists and Platonism in the Romantic period.

Sarah Hutton teaches at the University of Wales, Aberystwyth. Her main area of research is seventeenth-century intellectual history, with a special interest in the Cambridge Platonists. Her publications include *Anne Conway. A Woman Philosopher* (2004), *Newton and Newtonianism* (edited with James E. Force, 2004), *Platonism and the English Imagination* (edited with Anna Baldwin, 2004), and an edition of Ralph Cudworth's *Treatise Concerning Eternal and Immutable Morality* (1996). She is Director of the series International Archives in the History of Ideas.

Abbreviations

References to the works of Descartes, Spinoza and Leibniz are abbreviated as follows.

Descartes
References to the writings of Descartes in the form of, e.g., 'AT VII 232–3' (i.e. vol. VII, pp. 232–3), are to *Oeuvres de Descartes*, ed. Charles Adam and Paul Tannery (12 vols., revised edn, Paris: Vrin/CNRS, 1964–76). 'CSM' refers to the English translation by J. Cottingham, R. Stoothoff and D. Murdoch, *The Philosophical Writings of Descartes*, vols. I and II (Cambridge: Cambridge University Press, 1985), and 'CSMK' to vol. III, *The Correspondence*, by the same translators together with A. Kenny (Cambridge: Cambridge University Press, 1991). References to AT can be found in the margins of CSM and CSMK.

Spinoza
References to Spinoza in the form of, e.g., '*Opera* I 24–5' (i.e. vol. I, pp. 24–5) are to the edition of Carl Gebhardt (4 vols., Heidelberg: Carl Winters, 1925). References to the *Opera* for works written (or in the case of *Ethics* begun) by September 1665 can be found in the margins of Edwin Curley's authoritative English edition and translation of *The Collected Works of Spinoza*, vol. I (Princeton, NJ: Princeton University Press, 1985). In accordance with common practice, references to *Ethics* may be in the form of, e.g., 'IP44C1' (i.e., Part I, Proposition 44, Corollary 1). ('D' = 'Demonstration', 'S' = Scholium.)

Leibniz
References to Leibniz in the form of, e.g., 'G IV, 467' (i.e. vol. IV, p. 467) are to *Die philosophischen Schriften von Gottfried Wilhelm Leibniz*, edited by C. I. Gerhardt (Berlin, 1975–90; reprint, Hildesheim: Olms,

1965). 'L 390' (i.e. p. 390) refers to *Philosophical Papers and Letters*, trans. and ed. Leroy E. Loemker, 2nd edn. (Dordrecht and Boston: Reidel, 1969). 'W 104' (i.e. p. 104) refers to *Leibniz Selections*, ed. Philip P. Wiener (New York: Scribners, 1951). 'A VI, iv, 990' (i.e. series VI, vol. iv, p. 990) refers to *Sämtliche Schriften und Briefe*, edition of the Berlin Academy (Darmstadt and Berlin, 1923–). 'Gr 557' (i.e. p. 557) refers to *Textes inédits*, ed. Gaston Grua (Paris: Presses Universitaires de France, 1948). 'C 358–9' (i.e. pp. 358–9) refers to *Opuscules et fragments inédits de Leibniz*, ed. Louis Couturat (Paris, 1903; reprint, Hildesheim: Olms, 1966).

1

Introduction

MICHAEL AYERS

'RATIONALIST' AND 'RATIONALISM' are terms used in rather different ways
in different contexts, ethical, theological or metaphysical. In the historiography of philosophy 'rationalist' is commonly used for certain European
philosophers of the seventeenth century, and it is in that sense that it is
used here. The great 'rationalists' were Descartes, Spinoza, Malebranche
and Leibniz, and they are so called for their claim that human reason or
intellect can arrive at knowledge or understanding of at least some
features of reality that is not dependent on sense-experience, except in so
far as sense-experience may be required as a mental stimulus. (It will be
considered below, however, whether or not Spinoza made *quite* that
claim.) For a very long time modern general philosophy before Kant was
understood above all as an epistemological argument between rationalists and empiricists, 'empiricists' being philosophers in a tradition that
in one way or another subordinated reason to experience.

For several decades in the twentieth century, however, the distinction
that had commonly been employed as if it were an indispensable tool in
the historiography of philosophy fell profoundly out of fashion among
Anglophone historians of philosophy. The division between rationalists
and empiricists began to come under attack around the middle of the
century, and within a few years was widely regarded as an unfounded
construction of later theory, an imposed model of thesis and antithesis
prior to synthesis. There is, however, plenty of evidence that exponents
of the so-called 'New Philosophy' of the seventeenth century, although
(by definition) broadly in agreement in their opposition to scholastic
Aristotelianism and in their appreciation of the explanatory potential of
mechanistic and corpuscularian physical theory, nevertheless often saw

Proceedings of the British Academy, **149**, 1–14. © The British Academy 2007.

themselves as significantly divided on traditional, indeed ancient, lines between those who put their main trust in a divinely ordained correspondence between created nature and universal principles evident to human reason, and those who subordinated reason to the senses and experience at least with respect to the necessary conceptual 'materials' of reasoning and knowledge, and certainly with respect to our cognitive relation to the natural world.[1] That the New Philosophers should be divided in this way is not surprising. The formulation of a corpuscularian mechanism as an alternative to the Aristotelian view of the material world owed much to two ideas that, although compatible, had disparate, incompatible origins. One is the Platonic idea that geometry is a key to understanding the created universe that is directly accessible to reason. The other is ancient atomism, elaborated by the empiricists Epicurus and Lucretius as a satisfying, but consciously speculative, explanation of the world as we experience it. And although Stoic cosmology had few takers in the seventeenth century, the Stoics envisaged a route from sense-experience to a kind of rational understanding of nature that probably influenced such early modern empiricists as Bacon and Hobbes.

The historiographical and critical employment of the rationalist–empiricist distinction has, no doubt, often been crude, but its denigration has often been based on flimsy and specious interpretive argument. It has been thought, for example, that if a philosopher recognises that experiments are important in physics (as Descartes did), it must be wrong to classify him without qualification as a rationalist; or that if a philosopher believes that it is possible in principle to 'perceive' or grasp the intrinsic necessity of fundamental physical laws (as Hobbes and Locke did), or even if he simply recognises a synthetic *a priori* (as Locke did), then it is misleading to call him an empiricist. Both those who have deployed

---

[1] This point is argued at some length by Thomas Lennon, *The Battle of the Gods and the Giants: The Legacies of Descartes and Gassendi 1655–1715* (Princeton: Princeton University Press, 1993). Lennon's title is taken from Plato's metaphor at *Sophist* 246. For discussion of the corresponding ancient division to which Plato refers, see, for example, Michael Frede, 'An Empiricist View of Knowledge', in S. Everson (ed.), *Companions to Ancient Thought 1: Epistemology* (Cambridge: Cambridge University Press, 1990). See also M. Ayers, 'Theories of Knowledge and Belief', in D. Garber and M. Ayers (eds.), *The Cambridge History of Seventeenth-Century Philosophy* (Cambridge: Cambridge University Press, 1998), vol. II, pp. 1003–61.

the rationalist–empiricist division and those who have criticised it have been inclined to assume that the terms 'rationalist' or 'empiricist' apply to any philosopher just in so far as his or her theory fits some ideal template; and that we can have access to each ideal system by deducing it from one or two fundamental and defining 'rationalist' or 'empiricist' principles. It would, I believe, be better to think of 'rationalism' and 'empiricism' as the names of rival historic traditions rather than of ideal systems. The interest of Descartes's account of the epistemological role of experiments does not lie in its being some kind of falling away from 'rationalism' and concession to 'empiricism', but in the way in which the (by then, certainly) virtually unavoidable task of explaining the value of experiment in the investigation of nature was undertaken by one 'New Philosopher' writing in the broadly Platonic tradition. The result is different from the (equally problematic) explanation given by Hume, a sceptical empiricist. And it affords no support to the idea that, as a philosopher who accepted and attempted to explain the obvious value of experiments, rather than denying or ignoring their value, Descartes was somehow less rigorous or consistent a rationalist than he might have been.

In short, the so-called 'rationalists' do have something in common, as do the 'empiricists'. The great seventeenth-century rationalists worked (if heretically, and each in his own way and for his own reasons) within a heavily theologised Platonic tradition. Each found room and work for a set, or significant subset, of characteristically Platonic or Neoplatonic concepts and models. Their employment of these models involved giving a pivotal role to God both in the theory of being and in the theory of knowledge. The 'empiricists', Bacon, Gassendi, Hobbes, Locke and others, ignored or rejected these Platonic notions and looked back to a different, more naturalistic, also ancient tradition — above all to Epicurus and Lucretius (themselves deeply indebted to earlier thinkers), but more generally to the great, centuries-long argument between Epicureans and Stoics on the one side, and a variety of sceptics on the other. Descartes's *Meditations* is, among other things, an anti-empiricist tract, not just an anti-Aristotelian one, while Locke's *Essay* includes sustained argument, often overlooked, against Platonist theory. The existence of this division, however, does not preclude the possibility that some philosophers should have attempted some kind of synthesis, combining what they perceived as the truth in each approach. Indeed, that is just what one would expect, and no reason at all to deny that the division existed.[2]

There was an ancient link between empiricism and materialism, although the connection became fairly loose in the seventeenth century. The connection between Platonism and an immaterialist account of the rational soul was firmer — at any rate, if we except Spinoza's subtle ontology. It was accordingly characteristic of the seventeenth-century version of 'the battle between the gods and the giants' that Descartes presented his philosophy in *Meditations* around a proof, not only of God's existence, but of the immateriality and natural immortality of the soul; and that Locke's studied agnosticism on that issue was interpreted by at least some of his critics as unacknowledged materialism of the kind more openly espoused by Hobbes.

The present volume is intended as a contribution to the exploration and exposition of the common ground of the great early modern 'rationalist' theories, different as they are from one another in many respects. It is notable that standard and popular commentaries in English on early modern philosophical systems have offered little or no analysis of the relationship between the main rationalist theories and the mainstream Platonic tradition. That situation has been improved by some recent publications. Nevertheless, when invited to convene the Dawes Hicks Symposium of 2004 on behalf of the British Academy, I took the opportunity of asking two of the leading experts on seventeenth-century rationalist philosophy to join me in examining the connection between rationalism and Platonism, directly or indirectly. Both, I am pleased to say, agreed to do so. Each of us invited another speaker to open discussion of his paper, and their responses are included in the present volume. I hope that the result is half as rewarding to readers as the whole enterprise has been for at least this participant. All contributors to the Symposium, I believe, gained from the lively and stimulating discussions

[2] Although his epistemology is certainly 'empiricist', Berkeley is one of those who drew on both traditions, aiming to separate out the truth from the error in each (for discussion, see M. Ayers, 'Was Berkeley an Empiricist or a Rationalist?' in K. Winkler (ed.), *The Cambridge Companion to Berkeley* (Cambridge: Cambridge University Press, 2006), pp. 34–62.

that followed presentation of the papers, both in and out of the lecture room.

John Cottingham's paper sets out some of the Platonic strands in Descartes's cosmology, metaphysics and moral theory. But he is interested in them less as evidence of the sources of Descartes's thought than in their relation to its 'Janus-faced' character. For Descartes's philosophy, he argues, is deeply imbued with ancient and medieval views of humanity's place in the divine order and yet is also, to a significant extent, the harbinger of a quite different, 'modern' conception of a value-neutral and (apart from us) impersonal natural universe, knowledge and mastery of which is the key to the good life. Cottingham argues that the latter conception is confirmed by Descartes's notorious thesis (present, but not prominently, in his works) that the 'eternal truths' of logic, mathematics and mechanics are created by God, and so in some deep sense could have been otherwise, even though they appear to created human reason to be necessary and self-intelligible. Cottingham argues that the reason why God created these truths in their relation to human reason is something that lies beyond the scope of human reason. Consequently, 'the Cartesian universe structured by such truths must be understood as diverging even more widely from the Platonic paradigm of a straightforwardly rational and value-laden cosmos'. In this divergence, he suggests, Descartes's cosmology has moved a long way towards Hume's more 'modern' view that such laws of physics as are accessible to us are contingent regularities, whatever 'ultimate springs and principles' may lie behind them. Cottingham assigns the modern conception to a 'controlling' mindset that he finds dominant in Descartes's natural philosophy and account of physical law. The 'ancient' conception he associates with the characteristically Platonic and Augustinian 'contemplative' mindset more apparent in Descartes's metaphysics or 'first philosophy'. Cottingham goes on to consider how a tension between these two 'mindsets' is manifested in Descartes's ethics, and to suggest that it represents a certain opposition within our moral thinking still calling for resolution.

Douglas Hedley, while agreeing with much of Professor Cottingham's analysis, has some reasoned reservations. He distinguishes, with examples, between 'explicit' and 'implicit' Platonism, and ascribes the latter to Descartes. Hedley explains implicit Platonism as consisting in certain Platonic or Neoplatonic notions, such as the notion of Ideas or Archetypes in the mind of God, that had become fully incorporated in mainstream Christian thought largely through the authority of St Augustine. Consequently they could be adopted without any self-conscious alignment with a distinctively Platonic tradition. Hedley does not find anything 'Platonic' in Descartes's philosophy beyond such widely accepted ideas. He nevertheless judges that Descartes's implicit Platonic theology significantly distinguishes his natural philosophy from anything much like Hume's, even though (as Hedley agrees with Cottingham) the tendency of Cartesian physics to strip nature of value and purpose is opposed to a fundamental strand in traditional Platonism. Hedley also questions Cottingham's apparent assumption that Platonism, whether explicit or implicit, does not contain within itself the means of reconciling the 'controlling' and 'contemplative' mindsets. Plato himself, after all, saw contemplation as a necessary condition of well-chosen action, and later Platonists held similar views.

Dr Hedley's distinction between explicit and implicit Platonism is a helpful one, but it is arguable that Descartes's Platonism, if not as full-blooded (or as distinct from 'implicit Platonism') as it might have been, is nevertheless fully self-conscious. It is generally accepted that Descartes drew directly on Augustine, despite some protestations to the contrary in his letters. It seems unlikely that he would have lacked all knowledge of the relation of Augustine's philosophy to Platonism. That is not to deny that it is worth noting the extent to which Descartes chose to keep within the bounds of such originally Platonic theory as was commonly incorporated into a more general Christian worldview. It may be relevant that the potential readers that Descartes seems to have been particularly eager to convince were Jesuits, who looked to St Thomas rather than to St Augustine.

Hedley's point that Platonic philosophy, although it may emphasise the value of contemplation and *theoria* for its own sake, nevertheless assigns it great importance as a condition of wise action gives rise to the question whether any reasonably coherent philosophy *could* drive a principled division between the theoretical and practical such as might seem to be implied by Cottingham's conception of a tension between opposed mindsets. There were philosophers, for example Locke, who argued that theoretical knowledge or 'science' is probably beyond human beings, and who accordingly advocated in its place systematic experimental enquiry for practical ends. But Locke did not deny that theoretical knowledge would have had practical implications if it had been as attainable as the Cartesians supposed.

My own paper is an attempt to clarify the debated question of the relationship of Spinoza's metaphysics to the Platonic tradition. I try to set out some of the obstacles, as I see them, lying in the way of a clear understanding of Spinoza's philosophical position and of the significance of his employment of Platonic notions. There are at least three plausible, apparently different, ways of reading *Ethics*, none of which is obviously anachronistic. Spinoza has seemed to some to be focused on the same themes and issues as such earlier Jewish philosophers as Maimonides, whose work was evidently known to him — philosophers who were deeply influenced by Neoplatonic theory. On the other hand, Spinoza's name has always been linked to those of his contemporaries, Descartes and Hobbes, and much enlightening commentary has analysed the relationship of his thought to theirs — especially, with respect to metaphysics, to that of Descartes. As Cottingham's paper demonstrates, there is a significant overlap of Cartesian and Platonist theory. But Spinoza constructs his own monism and his critique of Cartesian philosophy by pursuing and interpreting a strand of Neoplatonist thought that Descartes leaves virtually undeveloped. I argue that Spinoza's hierarchical system of substance, attribute, immediate and mediate infinite modes, and, lastly, finite modes matches in some surprising respects Neoplatonist accounts of the emanation of the universe from God. I suggest that the comparison can throw light on the structure of Spinoza's monism and certain controversial issues of interpretation. But his bringing reinterpreted Neoplatonist ideas to bear against Descartes's pluralist metaphysics does not necessarily make him more of a Platonist than Descartes, since his version of those ideas, although expressed in Cartesian and theistic terms, is arguably so deeply naturalistic as to constitute a kind of subversion of Platonism as it had previously existed. Even Spinoza's epistemology, so I argue, for all its apparently Cartesian–Platonic structure, is seen on closer inspection to give sense, imagination and the body indispensable roles in both of the functions traditionally assigned to pure intellect, with respect to the possession both of universal knowledge and of self-knowledge. His explanation of the perception of universal and necessary principles, I suggest, might be thought to bring him closer to Hobbes than to Plato or Descartes. For Hobbes too, perhaps influenced by Bacon and Stoic theory, thought that we can perceive or grasp the necessary laws of mechanical physics by focusing on the common properties of the bodies perceived by sense.

This is the third way of reading Spinoza, as the philosopher who disenchants the Platonist's world by naturalising God, including God's epistemological role as the giver of light. The traditional view of Spinoza as an atheist and materialist may be a version of this reading that is too crude to be accurate, but the reading itself is the one most straightforwardly consonant with his theologically subversive interpretation of the Bible.

Sarah Hutton agrees with the identification of Platonist elements in Spinoza's metaphysics, but questions the claim that there are also elements tending to subvert the Platonist worldview. She begins by considering the question of the sources of Spinoza's Platonism or Neoplatonism, referring sympathetically to Richard Popkin's proposal that Spinoza was strongly influenced by certain Kabbalist ideas, themselves developed or interpreted under the influence of Neoplatonism. Although Spinoza's only extant reference to Kabbalism is contemptuous, Professor Hutton argues that the Kabbala constituted the only contemporary vehicle of Neoplatonist ideas that was widely known and discussed by Dutch Christian and Jewish intellectuals and scholars such as made up Spinoza's milieu. But she suggests that, whether it was Kabbalist or other Neoplatonic sources that were the important influence on Spinoza's thought, it is more plausible to read Spinoza as writing in the same essentially religious Platonist tradition than as the advocate of a naturalistic system essentially subversive of Platonism. She also brings against the latter interpretation the point that, in representing intellect as dependent for its subject-matter on the senses, Spinoza was not in fact straying from a traditional Platonist line of thought. She cites the epistemology of Plotinus as an example. Against the analogy with Hobbes, she argues that it is essential to Spinoza's explanation of how we are able to apprehend the 'Common Notions' generally and the laws governing perceived bodies in particular that, in doing so, our minds participate in the mind of God. Spinoza's three levels of knowledge, Hutton thinks, may be understood in an authentically Platonist way, with the highest level the furthest away from the mere deliverances of the senses, and the closest (to put it mildly) to the mind of God.

Neither Sarah Hutton nor I (I think) offer conclusive reasons for one rather than the other of our different readings of Spinoza. I find it inherently implausible that the kind of mystical hermeneutics and visionary religious ideas and language found in the Kabbala were what inspired Spinoza's austere, quasi-geometrical masterpiece — or even that they were a significant source of his knowledge of Neoplatonist ideas. Popkin's argument, at least, is too sketchy to carry conviction, although it is both interesting and understandable that Neoplatonism should have had a clearly discernible influence on such opposed styles of thought occurring around the same time. On the other hand, it is impossible simply to deny Professor Hutton's thesis that there 'is a sense in which Spinoza retains the Platonist epistemological doctrine of the participation of the mind in God'. The same goes for the point, made by both of us, that Spinoza's account of the different levels of knowledge — his 'stratification of knowledge' — echoes Platonist doctrine. With respect to the latter point, the question between us is, in effect, whether or not the echo is deliberately distorted in an unplatonic, sense-based direction. We disagree, I take it, not with respect to the existence both of similarities and of differences between Spinoza and Hobbes, and between Spinoza and such Neoplatonists as Plotinus, but with respect to the significance of those points of resemblance and difference. For example, is Spinoza's epistemological employment of the notion of the participation of finite minds in the mind of God deflationary, in that he gives the notion a naturalistic interpretation? Or does it have the opposite intention, comparably to Malebranche's thesis that we see all things in God? Perhaps that opposition is a little too sharp, and Professor Hutton would be satisfied with the possibility, raised by Robert Adams in discussion, that Spinoza was looking for a way to reconcile a naturalistic view of the world with a genuinely theistic and religious view of it, and that he saw a way of doing so within a Platonist framework. If, on the other hand, it is my suggestion that is correct, certain absolutely central features of

traditional Platonism constitute a main part of Spinoza's target, along
with anthropomorphism, the doctrine of free will, and revealed religion
in general, in his pursuit of a thoroughly naturalistic system. One of those
discarded features is the ontological priority of mind over matter.
Another is the Platonist view of the contribution of sense to the exercise
of reason or intellect, which for Plotinus as for Plato and Descartes is
contingent on the soul's embodiment in this life.

   None of the other leading rationalists are monists in the way of
Spinoza. They do not hold that everything finite and imperfect is liter-
ally contained within, or is a part of, what is infinite and perfect. Creator
and Creation, God and Nature, are kept apart in their systems.
Nevertheless they adopt, with Spinoza, what Robert Adams rightly identifies as a main theme of the Platonic tradition, the thesis that all things
are to be understood in terms of their relation to what is most perfect.
That principle can be taken in a merely causal sense, to the effect that all
things derive or flow intelligibly from the most perfect thing; or it can be
taken to mean that understanding what, for example, the finite goodness
of mundane particulars is, is posterior to understanding what perfect or
infinite goodness is. Professor Adams considers critically how far, and
how, the principle of the priority of the perfect understood in this second,
conceptual way was variously developed and explained by Descartes,
Spinoza and Leibniz. He moves on to consider whether there is any sense
in which the principle is actually defensible, whether by the arguments of
those philosophers or by further argument.

   Professor Adams sees this old idea, that the less perfect or complete
needs to be understood in terms of what is more perfect and complete
(the 'top-down' strategy), as one that is at least in some contexts at odds
with the rejection of Aristotelian science and the modern strategy of
explaining complex wholes in terms of simpler parts (the 'bottom-up'
strategy). In epistemology, empiricists such as Gassendi and Locke
argued that even our ideas of infinity and of the infinite attributes of God
are constructed from ideas of what is finite and given in experience.
Descartes, while favouring a bottom-up approach in explaining the
behaviour of complex physical objects, argued against it in natural
theology, holding, for example, that our idea of infinite being is positive,
whereas what distinguishes the finite from the infinite is limit, the nega-

tion of being. Moreover, the idea of being in general, he held, simply is the idea of infinite being. Adams discusses a number of problems for Descartes's position, suggesting, for example, that what prevented him from extending his arguments to all mundane attributes is that he held God to be incorporeal. Ideas of finite extension are therefore *not* constructible from the idea of an infinite attribute of God. Descartes's successors avoided this problem: Spinoza's God is extended, and Leibniz's extension is a merely phenomenal property.[3]

Because of his monism, Spinoza's approach is radically different from Descartes's in other respects. Finite things, in so far as we know them, are modes (that is, partial or determinate expressions) of the only divine attributes known to us, extension and thought. A mode, by definition, cannot be conceived of independently of the infinite attribute of which it is a mode. Adams explores the subtle and novel implications of Spinoza's position, for example that 'thought and extension are predicated univocally of finite things and God', and that a number of the traditional attributes of God are merely 'properties', since they do not pertain to God's positive essence. But it is in Leibniz's thinking on the subject that Adams finds the most promising material.

According to Adams, Leibniz develops the notion that those essential properties that constitute the *reality* of things owe their positive content to their relation to the attributes of God. Finite things do not just derive their existence from God, but owe their *realitas*, 'thingishness', to this relation between the absolute reality of God and the lesser, limited reality of creatures. The attributes of God are *perfections*, positive and absolute — that is to say, without limit. Moreover, they are simple, and so conceptually prior to whatever is complex, the concept of which involves

---

[3] Malebranche, whom Adams does not discuss, seems to have seen no such problem, at least none that could not be dealt with by insisting that, whenever we perceive any particular body, the idea of extension in general, i.e. of infinite extension, is present to us, subjected to limitation by sensation, a modification of the mind. Similarly, he held that when we think of a finite being, the idea of infinite being is before the mind. He evidently thought it enough to explain the positive infinity of our idea of extension to identify it with the *divine idea of extension*, revealed to us by God, even though it is not the *idea of divine extension*. Since he denies that we have access to an *idea* of mind or thought, it is our conception of divine, infinite mentality that must be constructed (i.e., by analogy with our own thought, of which we are reflexively conscious).

limitation or negation: 'On this view, the less than perfect properties of finite things must all be composed, by logical operations including various degrees of limitation or partial negation, from the simple perfections of God.' The problem with this view that Adams then identifies is that of how a *simple* perfection can be *partly* negated, since what is simple has no parts. He considers the proposal that comparatives supply what is needed: for example, human beings have *less than* the perfect power of God. But such comparative properties supervene on non-comparative, positive qualities, and the latter are not to be explained by the former. In the end, Adams concludes, this objection is fatal. Nevertheless he explores other ways of developing a top-down account on Leibnizian lines, without insisting on the simplicity of divine attributes. The best possibility, in Adams's view, can be illustrated by the idea that divine knowledge constitutes a kind of perfect ideal or archetype which human knowledge imperfectly resembles or approaches. Our knowledge and thought, he suggests, could be to God's rather as a dog's is to ours, and other 'perfections', such as substantiality, goodness and beauty, might be subject to similar treatment.

Maria Rosa Antognazza offers a critical commentary on Adams's discussion aimed at 'unpacking the significance, importance and, at the same time, difficulty of the "top-down" project' in philosophical theology. In the first part of her paper, she identifies the point of the project as a way of establishing that God's properties are the ontological grounding of the properties of finite things, in other words, that God is the root or ground of all reality — a conclusion not available to a bottom-up approach. According to the top-down argument, the postulation of an infinite being makes intelligible the finite objects of experience, whereas the bottom-up strategy works from what is given in experience without even assuming its intelligibility or ontological coherence.

In the second part of her paper, Dr Antognazza considers whether the theologically more promising top-down strategy does not simply beg a crucial question by assuming that we can have some conception of the perfect that is independent of, or prior to, a conception of the imperfect — in effect, conflating the postulated ontological priority of the perfect with epistemological priority. What reason have we to trust any reasoning about 'the most perfect being'? — the question raised by Leibniz's famous criticism of Descartes's ontological argument. Antognazza offers two ways in which the problem might be approached. First, there are traditional *a posteriori* proofs that something satisfies the predicates that define God, a most perfect being, which, if valid, afford the possibility of further reasoning that that thing is ontologically prior to whatever is imperfect and finite. Second, both Descartes and Leibniz operate with a notion of degrees of perception or knowledge, allowing that we have only an inadequate and confused idea of the perfect being, but one that is nevertheless clear and positive, and capable of being employed in reasoning. But again, if an idea is confused, it may hide a contradiction and be unfit to play a part in our reasoning.

In her third section, Antognazza asks in effect whether one should be satisfied with the conclusion that the thesis of the priority of the perfect is intelligible with respect only to *some* properties, such as the 'perfections' knowledge and goodness. If the top-down thesis is less than the claim that the most perfect being grounds *all* reality, it loses much of its theological interest. Only Spinoza, she thinks, succeeds in formulating a *general* top-down thesis, and the price is an immanent God, the merging of finite and infinite. Finally, Antognazza focuses on the topic of simplicity, and considers possible responses to Adams's argument that a simple property cannot be partly negated, since it has no parts. She suggests that Spinoza has a kind of answer to this problem in his conception of finite modes as partial expressions of simple and infinite attributes — but again at an ontological cost that Leibniz would not have been prepared to pay. But she concludes that the persistence of the Platonic 'top-down' tradition in theology is a mark of its continuing interest and promise.

Adams and Antognazza focus on the theological context, which is probably the one in which Platonism has had its most continuous life and influence, and the issues they identify are approached from a historical point of view. But what they say is of philosophical interest beyond that context, and should be so even for those who believe that natural theology is a branch of enquiry without an object. The theological arguments overlie issues about the relations between universal and particular, and between what is determinable and what is determinate, and about the ways in which these relations can vary depending on the kinds of concepts in question. Why is it the case, for instance, that, as Adams points out, the 'top-down' approach works most plausibly for what he calls 'perfections', finite examples of which seem merely to approach, without ever reaching, full instantiation of the property — without ever achieving absolute perfection in their kind? A possible analogy (the significance of which would appear to be confirmed by a genealogy of the Platonist position) is with geometrical concepts. 'Circle' and 'square' are predicates satisfied by some finite particulars, but physical instances always fall below the standard set by the perfect circle and square as treated in geometry. The notion of a perfect red, on the other hand, the red that sets a standard beyond the reach of any particular red thing, is rather more difficult to sustain. Such differences are surely of philosophical interest, whether or not we are inclined to link them to a question about God's role as the ultimate ground of reality.

2

Plato's Sun and Descartes's Stove: Contemplation and Control in Cartesian Philosophy

JOHN COTTINGHAM

Introduction

'LET NO ONE UNSKILLED IN GEOMETRY ENTER HERE'.[1] Descartes could have marched in boldly under the famous inscription over the portals of Plato's Academy, since, as Thomas Hobbes reportedly remarked, he was set to be one of the best geometers of his age, had he not been diverted into philosophy.[2] The cosmological system that Descartes produced was, like that of Plato, heavily dependent on geometrical and other mathematical ideas, both in its fine detail and in its general principles.[3] Also like Plato, Descartes believed in the unity of the sciences, as against the separatist Aristotelian view of a plurality of disciplines each with its own

---

[1] *Medeis ageômetretos eisitô.* The tradition that this phrase was inscribed over the portals of Plato's Academy has not been traced back further than Joannes Philoponus, a Neoplatonic Christian philosopher who lived in Alexandria in the sixth century AD. See H. G. Liddell and R. Scott-Jones, *A Greek English Dictionary*, rev. H. S. Jones (9th edn. Oxford: Clarendon Press, 1996), s.v. ἀγεῶμετρῆτος.

[2] According to John Aubrey, Thomas Hobbes 'would say that had [Des Cartes] kept himselfe wholly to Geometrie he had been the best Geometer in the world but that his head did not lye for Philosophy' (*Brief Lives* [c. 1680], ed. O. Lawson Dick (Harmondsworth: Penguin, 1962), p. 237.

[3] See René Descartes, *Rules for the Direction of our Native Intelligence [Regulae ad directionem ingenii, c.* 1628], Rule Four (AT X 376–8; CSM I 18–19); *Principles of Philosophy [Principia philosophiae,* 1644], Part II, art. 64 (AT VIIIA 78–9; CSM I 247). (For an explanation of references to the works of Descartes in this form, see Abbreviations, p. ix.)

Proceedings of the British Academy, **149**, 15–44. © The British Academy 2007.

methods and standards of precision.[4] Again, like Plato, he mistrusted and indeed repudiated the senses as a source of knowledge.[5] Finally, like Plato, Descartes argued for the immateriality of the soul and its resulting aptness to survive separation from the body;[6] and he wrestled with the implications of all this for the conduct of life.[7]

This is quite a list — and no doubt it could be augmented. And working with such a list, the historian of ideas could certainly construct a rich account of Platonic influences and sources for Cartesian philosophy, filling out the picture with reference not just to Plato's writings,[8] but to a host of texts from the succeeding centuries, from Plotinus to Augustine and on down to the Neoplatonists of the Renaissance. Descartes hated to acknowledge predecessors, and reacted with stiff defensiveness when asked about his debts (he was reluctant, for example, even to admit that his Cogito had been inspired by St Augustine).[9] But no philosopher, even the most original, creates out of nothing, and it is always interesting to uncover some of the ingredients of the process.

My own aim in this paper will, however, be somewhat different. I shall take in turn three principal areas of Cartesian philosophy, namely cosmology, metaphysics and morals, and in each case I shall identify some important strands in Descartes's thinking that may broadly be characterised as 'Platonic'. But I want to examine these not simply from the perspective of the history of ideas — with a view to uncovering

[4] See *Regulae* (AT X 378; CSM I 19); *Principles of Philosophy*, Preface to French translation of 1647 (AT IXB 14; CSM I 186).

[5] See, e.g., *Principles of Philosophy*, Part I, arts. 68 and 69 (AT VIIIA 33; CSM I 217).

[6] See *Meditations: Replies to Objections [Objectiones et Responsiones, 1641]*, Second Set (AT VII 153; CSM II 209). See also J. Cottingham, 'Cartesian Dualism: Theology, Metaphysics and Science', in J. Cottingham (ed.), *The Cambridge Companion to Descartes* (Cambridge: Cambridge University Press, 1992), ch. 8.

[7] See Letter to Elizabeth of 1 September 1645 (AT IV 286; CSMK 264–5).

[8] When one contrasts Plato's own texts with subsequent 'Platonic' interpretations, it should not be supposed that it is a straightforward matter to derive from those texts an original core of doctrines that represent Plato's own philosophical views. One of the hallmarks of a truly great philosopher is the way in which his writings attract diverse interpretations, and, as Myles Burnyeat has elegantly demonstrated, Plato is an 'extreme case' of this. See M. F. Burnyeat, 'Plato', *Proceedings of the British Academy*, vol. 111 (2001), pp. 1–22.

[9] See Letter to Colvius of 16 November 1640 (AT II 247–8; CSMK 159).

how Descartes drew on previous sources — but also with a partly proleptic eye, to see how (what we can now recognise as) Descartes's 'modernising' tendencies pulled him forwards and away from his classical and medieval forebears. This will in turn throw into focus the curiously problematic link that obtains between today's philosophical outlook and that of the so-called 'father' of the modern subject. Descartes has unavoidably become for us the archetypal Janus figure — the leading herald of our modern age whose thought was at the same time closely grafted onto the medieval and classical tradition that made it possible. By looking at our own relationship with him in this double light, by seeing both his proximity to us and his distance from us, we may perhaps gain a better sense of the distinctively philosophical (in contrast to the purely historical) point of studying his ideas. For in seeing which way Descartes himself turned (forwards or backwards, as it were) at certain crucial points in the development of his system, we may deepen our understanding of some of the tensions that still operate beneath the surface of our own contemporary philosophical worldview.

Cartesian Cosmology: from Order to Opacity

First, then, Descartes's cosmology. At least one commentator has recently drawn attention to possible links between the Cartesian theory of the physical universe and the Platonic cosmological tradition derived from the *Timaeus*, which had attracted considerable if sometimes erratic attention from assorted philosophical commentators in the centuries leading up to the early modern revolution.[10]

When in his first published work Descartes described the basic character of his cosmological outlook, he wrote the following:

> I noticed certain laws which God has so established in nature, and of
> which he has implanted such notions in our minds, that after adequate

[10] See Catherine Wilson, 'Soul, Body, and World' in S. Hutton and D. Hedley (eds.), *Platonism at the Origins of Modernity* (Dordrecht: Springer, 2007, pp. 177–91).

reflection we cannot doubt that they are exactly observed in everything
that exists or occurs in the world.[11]

The claim is the powerful one that the human mind is a divinely certified
'mirror of nature'.[12] In creating us, God structured our minds in such a
way as to reflect the selfsame rationally accessible parameters that operate in his other creation — the material universe. It is this match that ultimately makes science possible, since the 'external' rationality manifest in
the created cosmos and the internal rationality of the human mind both
stem from the same divine creator. Now, according to Stephen Menn, in
his justly admired study of Descartes and Augustine, this is precisely the
picture we find in Plato's *Timaeus:*

> [For Plato] the world is governed by an intrinsically rational divine power,
> and this power is the source of rational order to the things it governs . . .
> Heraclitus calls the source of rationality *logos*; Plato follows Anaxagoras
> in calling it *nous* . . . Plato builds the physics of the *Timaeus* on this
> hypothesis, and the divine demiurge of that dialogue is identical with the
> world-governing *nous* that Plato invokes in the *Philebus* and also in
> passages of the *Laws* . . . Nous is able to order the world, causing
> different portions of matter to participate in different intelligible forms
> at different times, according to a single all-encompassing rational
> pattern.[13]

It is not hard to see how there could be a fairly smooth transition
between the Platonic cosmos so described and the Christian conception
of a divine rationality at the heart of creation: 'In the beginning was
the *logos*'. In the opening chapter of the Fourth Gospel, the *logos* is of
course famously associated with light. And certainly in Descartes, the
new science seems to be predicated on the idea of the divine light of

---

[11] 'J'ai remarqué certaines loix, que Dieu a tellement établies en la nature, et dont il a
imprimé de telles notions en nos âmes, qu'après y avoir fait assez de réflexion, nous ne
saurions douter qu'elle ne soient exactement observées, en tout ce qui est ou qui se fait
dans le monde.' *Discourse on Method* [*Discours de la méthode*, 1637], part v (AT VI 41;
CSM II 131).
[12] For this phrase (albeit used in a wider sense), cf. Richard Rorty, *Philosophy and the
Mirror of Nature* (Oxford: Blackwell, 1980).
[13] Stephen Menn, *Descartes and Augustine* (Cambridge: Cambridge University Press,
1998), pp. 87–8.

reason, manifest in the workings of the material universe, and illuminating the minds of the human scientists who investigate its structure. This is not of course to say that there are not many important differences between Plato, St John and Descartes. The standard Christian picture, adopted by Descartes, is of divine creative responsibility for all there is ('without Him was not anything made that was made' — John 1:3): we have creation *ex nihilo*, rather than (as in Plato) the demiurge ordering of a pre-existing chaos. So while Plato can retain a dualistic picture, with a residual imperfection, a kind of raw unruliness of matter, set over against the divine impulse of rationality and order, Descartes as a Christian philosopher will follow the uncompromising Augustinian line: there is but one source of reality, and the explanation for any defects will have to be sought elsewhere.[14] But despite this and other important differences, the parallel emphasised by Descartes in the *Discourse* between the divine ordering of the external universe and the ordering of the human mind seems to be appropriately characterised as a genuinely Platonic idea.[15]

This impression of continuity appears to be reinforced when we look at Descartes's earlier suppressed work, *Le Monde*, written only five years or so before the *Discourse*. For there an initial chaos makes its appearance; this is not, to be sure, as Plato's is, independent of or prior to God — but none the less it does not intrinsically possess any order until, 'from the first instant of creation', God imparts certain motions into the parts of matter. Having done so,

> he causes these parts to continue moving thereafter in accordance with the

[14] In particular, for Augustine, in the bad use of our free will: 'everything called "evil" is either sin, or the penalty of sin' (*De Genesi ad litteram imperfectus liber* [393 CE], i, 3); 'the cause of evil is the defection of the will of a being who is mutably good from the Good which is immutable' (*Enchiridion* [423 CE], viii, 23). Descartes adapts this theodicy in explaining the cause of epistemic error in the Fourth Meditation (AT VII 56ff.; CSM II 39ff.).

[15] There are, inevitably, some caveats, the most significant of which was made by the great Plato scholar F. M. Cornford, who cautioned against an over-Christianised reading of the *Timaeus*: 'It is not fair either to Plato or to the New Testament to ascribe the most characteristic revelations of the Founder of Christianity to a pagan polytheist' (*Plato's Cosmology*, London: Routledge, 1937, p. 35). Cornford stresses that it is nowhere suggested that the demiurge should be an object of worship: 'he is not a religious figure' (*ibid.*).

ordinary laws of nature. For God has established those laws in such a
marvellous way that . . . they are sufficient to cause the parts of this chaos
to disentangle themselves and arrange themselves in such good order that
they will have the form of a quite perfect world.[16]

The picture looks at first to be broadly in harmony with both Plato and
indeed the account in Genesis. An initial chaos — the world is *tohu
bohu* — formless (Genesis 1:2); and then the voice of God is heard and a
perfect world is formed: 'and God saw that it was very good' (1:31).[17] Or
in Plato's *Timaeus*: 'As our world is the fairest of things that have come
into being (*kallistos tôn gegonotôn*) so God is the best of causes (*aristos
tôn aitiôn*); having come into being in this way, the world was fashioned
according to what is graspable by rationality and intelligence.'[18]

Yet despite the parallels just noted (and now I come, as it were, to the
antithesis), a closer scrutiny finds in Descartes passages that point in
quite a different direction, prefiguring the bleaker, ethically blank universe so typical of our modern scientific world picture. Pascal famously
said that he could not forgive Descartes for reducing God's role to that of
giving the system an initial shove.[19] That particular criticism is in fact
misconceived since Cartesian matter, being pure geometrical extension,
has no power of its own to transmit, or continue in, motion; hence the
motive power of God is continuously required to conserve as well as to
create the motion in the cosmos.[20] But Pascal's general sense that the
Cartesian deity is somehow remote in comparison to the living God of
religious tradition none the less carries more than a germ of truth. The
key to this lies in Descartes's remark (quoted above) that the different-
sized particles of varying shapes that compose the initial matter of the
universe are given certain initial motions and then caused to continue

---

[16] *The World* [*Le Monde*, 1633], ch. 6 (AT XI 34; CSM I 91).
[17] The Septuagint translation of Genesis uses the term *cosmos* to convey this order and
goodness of the created universe: 'the heaven and the earth and the whole *cosmos* of
them' (Genesis 2:1).
[18] Plato, *Timaeus* [*c.* 360 BCE], 29A; my translation.
[19] 'Je ne puis pardonner à Descartes: il voudrait bien dans toute la philosophie se pouvoir
passer de Dieu; mais il n'a pu s'empêcher de lui donner une chiquenaude pour mettre le
monde en mouvement; après cela, il n'a plus que faire de Dieu.' Blaise Pascal, *Pensées*
[*c.* 1660], ed. L. Lafuma (Paris: Seuil, 1962), no. 1001.
[20] See *Principles of Philosophy*, part II, art. 36 (AT VIIIA 61; CSM I 240).

moving thereafter 'in accordance with the ordinary laws of nature' (*suivant les lois ordinaires de la Nature*). Although Descartes does not put it this way (and although, as just noted, the divine action is needed to conserve motion), none the less the thought has been planted that all one needs in order to provide an adequate explanation for the cosmos as we now find it is a set of initial conditions specifying certain quantities of matter in motion (its particles defined in terms of size and shape), plus certain universal laws governing the subsequent movement of those particles.[21]

Although the *result* of the operation of these laws may be the magnificent universe we now observe — galaxies, stars, planets — the laws themselves do not appear to manifest any particular beauty (apart, perhaps, from their mathematical simplicity), nor indeed any intrinsic design or purposiveness. Isaac Newton, whose mathematical physics was in due course to supersede that of Descartes (and who adapted to his purposes some elements of the Cartesian system, for example the principle of rectilinear inertial motion), did indeed subscribe to the idea of design, observing that 'The most beautiful system of the sun, planets and comets could only proceed from the counsel and dominion of an intelligent and powerful Being [whom we know] by his most wise and excellent contrivances of things, and final causes . . .'[22] But Newton's reasoning for this invocation of divine ordering was that he believed that some kind of supernatural intervention would be needed to correct the celestial motions that would otherwise be perturbed as a result of the operation of gravity:

> I do not think [the solar system] explicable by mere natural causes, but am forced to ascribe it to the counsel and contrivance of a voluntary agent . . .
> Gravity may put the planets into motion, but without the divine power it could never put them into such a Circulating motion as they have about

[21] Descartes reduces these laws to three — the principle of inertia, the principle of rectilinear motion, and the principle of the conservation of quantity of motion: *Principles*, part II, arts. 37–40. For some contrasts between Descartes's system and the ancient atomism which it in some respects resembles, see *Principles*, part IV, art. 202.

[22] *Philosophiae naturalis principia mathematica* [1687], trans. A. Motte (London, 1729), pp. 344–6.

the Sun, and therefore for this as well as other reasons I am compelled to ascribe the frame of this System to an intelligent Agent.[23]

The counterfactual corollary is apparent: *were* it ever to turn out to be the case that one could, e.g. by modifying the theory of gravity or in some other way, discover a natural explanation for the actual perturbations of motions found in the solar system, then the intelligent interventions would be redundant.[24] But what at all events seems to be implicitly conceded by Newton in this passage is that the mere system of gravitational bodies moving subject to the law of inertial motion plus the inverse square law does not itself require a divine orderer, at any rate not in the sense of a purposive intelligence; the general pattern is, as it were, derived simply from the natural disposition of things, explicable by 'mere natural causes'.

Talk of Newtonian forces like gravitation of course takes us beyond Descartes's frame of reference; but the general point applicable to the Cartesian cosmological system remains. The universe that Descartes describes in *Le Monde* is not presented as possessing the kind of order that requires us to invoke a supernatural intelligence; rather, if we take it as axiomatic that particle interactions operate in accordance with the mathematical covering laws specified by Descartes in *Le Monde* and later in his *Principia philosophiae*, then we have, as it were, all that is needed to explain the natural world as we find it. The position is summed up in the opening paragraph of chapter 7 of *Le Monde* (although the language, which Descartes eventually decided should not see the light of day, is considerably more forthright than he later felt able to use when he published the *Principles*):

> By 'nature' here I do not mean some goddess or any other sort of imaginary power. Rather, I am using this word to signify *matter itself*, in so far as I am considering it taken together with all the qualities I have attributed to it, and under the condition that God continues to preserve it in the same way that he created it. For it follows of necessity, from the mere fact that he continues thus to preserve it, that there must be many changes in its

[23] Letters to Bentley of 10 December 1692 and 17 January 1693.
[24] The more sophisticated system of Einstein (which encompasses perturbations unexplained in the Newtonian cosmos) arguably achieves just such completeness.

parts which cannot, it seems to me, properly be attributed to the action of God (because His action never changes), and which therefore I attribute to nature. The rules by which the changes take place I call the 'laws of nature'.[25]

Not only is there explicit rejection of the need for any Platonic-style animating intermediaries (such as the 'world-soul' found in the *Timaeus* and in many Neoplatonic writings), but the divine presence in nature is reduced to a minimum; there seems to be more than a hint here of what will become the orthodox modern conception of physics, that the system of nature is pretty much autonomous, nothing more or less than 'matter itself', operating in accordance with suitably described covering principles. We are thus by now quite far away from the Christianised Platonism that was so vividly alive three centuries earlier, when Dante wrote:

> Le cose tutte quante
> hanno l'ordine tra loro, e questo è forma
> che l'Universo a Dio fa simigliante.
> Qui veggion l'alte creature l'orma
> de l'eterno valore, il quale è fine
> al quale è fatta la toccata norma.

> All things that do exist
> have order deep within, which is the form
> that makes the Universe like unto God.
> The higher creatures see in them the stamp
> of value everlasting, the true end
> for which this rule and order was decreed.[26]

---

[25] '[P]ar la Nature je n'entends point ici quelque Déesse, ou quelque autre sorte de puissance imaginaire, mais . . . je me sers de ce mot pour signifier la Matière même en tant que je la considère avec toutes les qualités que je lui ai attribuées comprises toutes ensemble, et sous cette condition que Dieu continue de la conserver en la même façon qu'il l'a créée. Car de cela seul qu'il continue ainsi de la conserver, il suit de nécessité qu'il doit y avoir plusieurs changements en ses parties, lesquels ne pouvant, ce me semble, être proprement attribués à l'action de Dieu, parce qu'elle ne change point, je les attribue à la Nature; et les règles suivant lesquelles se font ces changments, je les nomme les lois de la Nature.' *Le Monde*, ch. 7 (AT XI 37; CSM I 92–3).

[26] Dante Alighieri, *La Divina Commedia: Paradiso* [*c*. 1300], canto I.

Dante's universe is alive with the beauty and order of its creator, rather like that later conceived by Leibniz, in which there is 'nothing waste, nothing sterile, nothing dead; no chaos, no confusions, save in appearance'.[27] In the Cartesian picture, by contrast, the world is a neutral, inanimate, purely mechanical plenum, with even the biological domain reduced to a series of particle interactions that Descartes himself firmly proclaimed to be no different in kind from what occurs in any other part of the physical universe.[28]

There is, however, a final question to be raised by way of postscript before we move on from Descartes's physics to other aspects of his system. I have argued that, despite initial Platonic echoes, the general tenor of Cartesian cosmology is better seen as pointing forward than backward, to the autonomous physics of modernity rather than to the value-laden cosmos of the *Timaeus*. But a possible objection to this 'autonomising' interpretation of Cartesian physics runs as follows: does not the mere fact of a law-like, mathematically describable universe tend to support the idea of rationality rather than randomness, of intelligence rather than blind evolution, of *logos* rather than *tyche*? Descartes may have banished beauty, design and finality from his physical cosmology,[29] but does not his firm commitment to the mathematicisation of physics in itself constitute adherence to the idea of the ultimate rationality of the universe and its creator?

This is, I think, a difficult question to answer, partly because modern philosophical debate has not really settled the question of whether the fine mathematical tuning of the cosmos is a deeply significant fact about its ultimate nature, perhaps even its divinely sourced nature, or merely (in Kantian spirit) a fact about the structure of the human mind, or again,

[27] G. W. Leibniz, *Monadology* [*Monadologie*, 1714], §69.

[28] 'I will try to give such a full account of the entire bodily machine that we will have no more reason to think that it is our soul which produces in it the movements which we know by experience are not controlled by our will than we have reason to think that there is soul in a clock which makes it tell the time.' *Description of the Human Body* [*La Description du corps humain*, 1647/8], part I (AT XI 226; CSM I 315). Compare also *Treatise on Man* [*L'Homme*, c. 1630], AT XI 202; CSM I 108.

[29] For Descartes's resolute rejection of finalism in science, see for example the Fourth Meditation: 'I consider the customary search for final causes to be totally useless in physics' (AT VII 55; CSM II 39).

more prosaically still, simply a banal truth about the contingent regularities that are a *sine qua non* for our being here to investigate them in the first place.[30] But if we keep the focus on Descartes himself, then there is a special complicating factor to be taken into account, namely his famous, or notorious, doctrine of the divine creation of the eternal truths — the doctrine, consistently maintained by Descartes, that God is the author of the truths of logic and mathematics, creating them by a sovereign act of will similar to that whereby He creates the material universe: He was wholly free to do otherwise.[31] This doctrine introduces a 'worm of contingency' into the Cartesian system.[32] For on Descartes's picture, although our minds are so structured that we cannot conceive of the eternal laws of mathematics as being otherwise, they remain, from God's perspective, wholly contingent on His creative will. It follows from this that the talk of a match between the human mind and the divine is in one sense misleading. We may have a clear and distinct grasp of the fundamental logical and mathematical principles by which the universe operates (as proclaimed in the resounding opening to Part Five of the *Discourse* with which we began this section), and in this sense we may think of the human mind as a mirror of nature. But because these truths are contingent on the divine will, the ultimate rationale for them, if any, must remain opaque to us. We cannot possibly conceive what it would be to create a logical or mathematical truth by an act of will, nor indeed how a truth so created could be a truth of reason in the sense in which we

[30] The significance of the so-called 'anthropic principle' is still a subject of fierce debate. For a theistic/design interpretation, compare the following: 'If we must make a forced choice between an unintelligent random process and an invisible Intelligence behind the scenes, as it appears we must, and if, furthermore, the chance against a random process accounting for the precise values of the basic constants of physics is well in excess of a billion to one, then a designer may be considered highly probable. In other words, the anthropic principle looks as if it might succeed . . . in making highly probable the existence of a universal designer–creator' (L. Stafford Betty with B. Cordell, 'The Anthropic Teleological Argument', *International Philosophical Quarterly*, 1987).
[31] See letters to Mersenne of 6 May 1630 and 27 May 1630 (AT I 150, 152; CSMK 24, 25). It has to be said, however, that Descartes did not give the doctrine much prominence in his major published works.
[32] Cf. J. Cottingham, 'The Cartesian legacy', *Proceedings of the Aristotelian Society*, supp. vol. LXVI (1992), pp. 1–21.

humans recognise such truths (namely as objects of thought that con-
strain the assent willy-nilly).[33]

The upshot is that the Cartesian universe structured by such truths
must be understood as diverging even more widely from the Platonic
paradigm of a straightforwardly rational and value-laden cosmos. The
Cartesian scientist is in no position to apprehend the ground or basis for
the universe's being the way it is: the rationale for the principles or laws
of motion must be, as Descartes said of all God's purposes, ultimately
'shut up in the inscrutable abyss' that is the mind of God.[34] And the cash
value of all this is that in the Cartesian system we have a worldview not
all that different from the one envisaged by David Hume, when he said
that the 'ultimate springs and principles of nature' must remain forever
'shut up from human curiosity'.[35] What Hume and Descartes in effect
agree on is that the human intellect is capable of arriving at principles of
maximum simplicity and generality which provide a framework for sub-
suming an indefinite range of observable phenomena.[36] But behind this

[33] For an elegant development of this point, see S. Gaukroger, *Cartesian Logic* (Oxford:
Clarendon Press, 1989), ch. 2.
[34] 'We cannot pretend that certain of God's purposes are more out in the open than
others: all are equally hidden in the inscrutable abyss of his wisdom' (Fifth Replies: AT
VII 375; CSM II 258). Compare *Conversation with Burman* [1648], ed. J. Cottingham
(Oxford: Clarendon Press, 1976), pp. 19, 85 (AT V 158; CSMK 341).
[35] '[T]he utmost effort of human reason is to reduce the principles productive of natural
phenomena to a greater simplicity and to resolve the many particular effects into a few
general causes . . . But as to the causes of these general causes, we should in vain attempt
their discovery . . . These ultimate springs and principles are totally shut up from human
curiosity and enquiry.' *Enquiry concerning Human Understanding* [1748], sect. 4, part i.
[36] This is not to deny important divergences between the Cartesian and Humean perspec-
tives on science: Hume's scientific methodology, for example, involves generalising from
experienced particulars, while Descartes claims that at least some laws can be arrived at
a priori. (It is worth noting, however, that Descartes does allow a considerable role for
empirical hypothesis when it comes to finding the correct explanations for particular
phenomena — a fact often ignored by those who caricature him as an 'armchair rationalist'. Cf. *Discourse on Method*, part vi: 'The power of nature is so vast, and [my] principles so simple and so general, that I notice hardly any effect of which I do not know
at once that it can be deduced from the principles in many different ways — and my
greatest difficulty is usually to know in which of these ways it depends on them. I know
of no other means to discover this than by seeking further observations whose outcomes
vary according to which of these ways provides the correct explanation' (AT VI 64–5;
CSM I 144).)

remarkable systematising success of human science lies what must remain for us a mere fiat: God simply willed, let it be thus and so. Beyond that, we cannot go. It is here that the Cartesian view of the status of human science goes a fair way to converging with our modern, post-Humean one: the gap between acknowledging an inscrutable divine fiat and simply accepting the unexplained explanatory postulates of modern secular physics seems to be wafer thin.

Metaphysics and the Return to God

The picture I have so far presented is, I think, accurate as far as it goes, but it now needs to be supplemented. I have just suggested that the divergence between the cosmological structure of Cartesian and of modern science is minimal. Epistemically speaking that may be more or less right; but ontologically speaking there is of course a crucial difference: whatever we may make of the precise significance of the deity within the Cartesian system, there is no doubt that Descartes, unlike his modern scientific successors, does explicitly assign an essential role to God as the source of all reality and truth. And if we go on to probe the metaphysical roots of Descartes's system, there is an even greater sense of divergence between the Cartesian and the modern picture. In Cartesian natural philosophy, there are distinct traces of Platonism, but I have suggested that they turn out under examination to be largely superficial; when we move to Cartesian first philosophy, by contrast,[37] the Platonism is powerfully integrated into the very structure of the thinking.

The journey recounted in Descartes's metaphysical masterpiece is too well known to need rehearsing at any length. At the start of the *Meditations*, the metaphysical enquirer follows the guidance of Plato in undergoing a process of *aversio*, or turning away from the senses, and in his struggle to find a way out of the Cave, or what Descartes calls the 'inextricable darkness' of the sense-bound world,[38] he takes the

[37] The term 'first philosophy' is of course the traditional Aristotelian term for metaphysics (see Aristotle, *Metaphysics* [*c*. 330 BCE], book gamma, 1004a9). The original title of Descartes's metaphysical meditations is *Meditationes de prima philosophia*.
[38] 'inextricabiles tenebrae' (AT VII 23; CSM II 15).

particular version of the Platonic journey that was pioneered by
Augustine, and looks for the truth deep within his own soul: *in interiore
homine habitat veritas*.[39] There follows, in the Third Meditation, an argument the terms of which (as one commentator has aptly remarked)[40]
unmistakeably 'manifest its Plotinian and Augustinian ancestry':

> I perceive this likeness, which includes the idea of God, by the same
> faculty which enables me to perceive myself. That is, when I turn my
> mind's eye upon myself, I understand that I am a thing which is incom-
> plete and dependent on another and which aspires without limit to ever
> greater and better things; but I also understand at the same time that he on
> whom I depend has within him all those greater things, not just indefinitely
> and potentially, but actually and infinitely, and hence that he is God.[41]

In the long discussion leading up to this conclusion, Descartes has
invoked an explicitly Platonic idea (expressed in the terminology of
Plotinus), observing that an investigation of the cause of his idea of God
must sooner or later lead him to a primary idea, 'the cause of which will
be like an *archetype* which contains formally and in fact all the reality or
perfection present only objectively or representatively in the idea'.[42] The
standard move we find in Plato is, for example, from particular beautiful
objects, mere shadows or copies, to an archetype or pattern or form or
idea of beauty itself; the Cartesian move here is from a mental object
(somewhat confusingly called an 'idea'[43]) — a mental object with a certain representative content — to the original of which it is a copy. And

---

[39] 'Noli foras ire, in teipsum redi; in interiore homine habitat veritas' ('Go not outside, but
return within thyself; in the inward man dwelleth the truth') *De vera religione* [AD 391],
XXXIX 72.
[40] Menn, *Descartes and Augustine*, p. 288.
[41] AT VII 51; CSM II 35.
[42] AT VII 42; CSM II 29 (emphasis supplied). The word 'archetype' (ἀρχέτυπον) does
not actually occur in Plato, though it aptly conveys the role of a Platonic form as pattern
or original (e.g. *Republic* [c. 380 BC], 510ff., 597ff.), and is found frequently in Plotinus
(*Enneads* [c. AD 250], 1.2.2 *et passim*), and in later writers in the Platonic tradition.
[43] Confusion might arise if the reader mistakenly equated it with a Platonic form, or with
a purely psychological item of the kind often associated with Locke's use of the term. For
the mistaken tendency of commentators to 'psychologise' Cartesian ideas, cf. J.
Cottingham, '"The only sure sign . . ." Descartes on Thought and Language', in J. M.
Preston (ed.), *Thought and Language* (Cambridge: Cambridge University Press, 1998),
pp. 29–50, esp. § 2.

echoing the broadly Platonic idea of a downward cascade of being from perfection to the lower realms, Descartes reminds us that 'the copy is like an image which can fall short of the perfection of the original but can never contain anything greater or more perfect'.[44] In inferring a divine source for the perfection found in his idea, Descartes (as Stephen Menn nicely puts it) 'confirms, for the case of Nous itself but not for the case of other particular *noeta* or Forms, the conclusion which [Plato in] the *Phaedo* had assumed . . . to hold in every case, that the ideal standard essentially possessing each intelligible perfection must exist in actuality.'[45]

Although the Platonic influences here are significant, it is not my purpose, as I remarked at the outset, to unravel the story of their transmission. And in the end, the occurrence of terminology which derives from a particular school of philosophy does not in itself tell us very much about its underlying philosophical (as opposed to historical) importance. Certainly in the Third Meditation the language suddenly becomes saturated with terminology that bears the imprint of the curriculum Descartes had studied at La Flèche; but for every one Platonic resonance one could undoubtedly cite two or three pieces of characteristically scholastic terminology whose ultimate begetter is not Plato but Aristotle. Nevertheless, we cannot avoid recognising how the Platonic language does indeed become prominent at key points in the development of Descartes's argument; and what seems to me crucial for understanding the relationship between the Cartesian outlook and our own contemporary worldview is the mindset that such language betrays — a mindset that can best be labelled *contemplative* as opposed to *controlling*.

Descartes's attraction to a contemplative mode of philosophising becomes perhaps most unmistakeable in the Fourth Meditation, where, in

---

[44] Third Meditation, AT VII 42; CSM II 29.

[45] Menn, *Descartes and Augustine*, p. 293. Some of the Neoplatonic developments of this idea (for example in Marsilio Ficino) are explored by Richard Popkin: 'Ficino tried to show that by contemplation we can reach illumination from Platonic ideas, thereby approaching ultimate knowledge, which is knowledge of God.' *The Cambridge History of Renaissance Philosophy*, ed. C. B. Schmitt and Q. Skinner (Cambridge: Cambridge University Press, 1988), p. 674.

a strongly Platonic moment, we are presented with a match between how the mind responds to the *ratio veri* and to the *ratio boni*.[46] The metaphysical journey from darkness and confusion to divine illumination, whether in the pursuit of truth or of goodness, involves a cooperation between intellect and will: the will must be exercised first in rejecting what is doubtful and unreliable, and then in focusing attention on the innate indubitable deliverances of the natural light that remain. Once the eye of the soul, the *acies mentis*, is turned on the relevant objects, they reveal themselves with irresistible clarity to the perceiving intellect as good or as true, and the assent of the will (to affirm, or to pursue) follows automatically: *ex magna luce in intellectu sequitur magna propensio in voluntate*.[47]

The history of the underlying visual metaphor for intellectual illumination is well known; the pedigree, with its roots in Plato and also in the Fourth Gospel, stretches down, via Plotinus, to Augustine, and on through to Bonaventure and beyond.[48] Descartes in fact directly follows Bonaventure in maintaining that the key to true illumination is the exercise of the will operating in conjunction with the light of the intellect. Our freedom of the will, in respect of which (Bonaventure and Descartes agree) man is truly godlike, consists, in Bonaventure's phrase, in a *concursus rationis et voluntatis*;[49] and this cooperation

---

[46] My spontaneous inclination to assent to the truth, or to pursue the good, is a function of my 'clearly understanding that reasons of truth and goodness point that way' (*quia rationem veri et boni in ea [parte] evidenter intelligo*); AT VII 58; CSM II 40.

[47] AT VII 59; CSM II 41.

[48] Plato, in the *Republic* [*c*. 380 BC] had used the simile of the sun to describe the Form of the Good which makes manifest the objects of abstract intellectual cognition, just as the sun sheds light on ordinary visible objects (514–18). In St John's Gospel [*c*. AD 100], the logos, the 'Word' or divine creative intelligence, is identified with 'the Light that lighteth every man coming into the world' (1:9). And Augustine, in the *De Trinitate* [*c*. 410], welding together Platonic and Christian ideas, asserts that 'the mind, when directed to intelligible things in the natural order, according to the disposition of the Creator, sees them in a certain incorporeal light which has a nature all of its own, just as the body's eye sees nearby objects in the ordinary light' (XII xv 24).

[49] 'Ex concursu illarum potentiarum, rationis supra se ipsam redeuntis et voluntatis concomitantis, consurgit integritas libertatis.' *Breviloquium* [1257], II ix; in *Opera Omnia* (Collegium S. Bonaventurae: Quaracchi, 1891), V 227b. Cf. E. Gilson, *La Philosophie de Saint Bonaventure* [1924], trans. I. Trethowan and F. J. Sheed (London: Sheed & Ward, 1938), p. 407.

between intellect and will brings the quest for enlightenment to fruition: *nata est anima ad percipiendum bonum infinitum, quod Deus est; ideo in eo solo debet quiescere et eo frui.*[50] The rational soul finds salvation in the intellectual awareness of an object, the turning of the will towards that object, and the happiness of satisfied desire that comes to rest in it.[51]

The language of the soul's coming to rest in adoring contemplation of the light is one we associate more with the early Middle Ages than with the early modern revolution, but such language still has an important place in Descartes. *Placet hic aliquamdiu in ipsius Dei contemplatione immorari . . . et immensi hujus luminis pulchritudinem . . . intueri, admirari, adorare* ('Let me here rest for a while in the contemplation of God himself and gaze upon, wonder at, and adore the beauty of this immense light').[52] The meditator's voice here in the Third Meditation is the voice of the worshipper (or perhaps of the philosopher in the Platonic sense that implies a genuine love or yearning) rather than of the analytic philosopher; or perhaps we should more aptly say that Descartes is adopting a modality of thought vividly exemplified in the writings of many of the Christian Fathers (Anselm particularly comes to mind)[53] — a mode in which analytic philosophising and religious contemplation are inextricably intertwined. The tone and impetus of the meditating are less of critical scrutiny than of humble submission. Just as for Augustine no salvation was possible without the gift of divine grace, so the scientific truth that Descartes seeks is dependent from the start on the 'immense light', mirrored in each individual soul,[54] or (to change the metaphor) on the idea of God being stamped there like the 'mark the craftsman has set on

---

[50] *Commentarii Sententiarum Petri Lombardi* [1248–55], bk. I, 1 iii 2 (*Opera* I, 40); cited in Gilson, *La Philosophie de Saint Bonaventure*, p. 89.

[51] *Ibid.*, p. 47.

[52] AT VII 52; CSM II 36.

[53] Cf. G. Schufreider, *Confessions of a Rational Mystic* (West Lafayette, IN: Purdue University Press, 1994).

[54] For the light mirrored within each soul, see Bonaventure, *Itinerarium mentis in Deum* [1259], III 1: 'ad nos reintraremus, in mentem scilicet nostram, in qua divina relucet imago; hinc . . . conari debemus per speculum videre Deum, ubi ad modum candelabri relucet lux veritatis in facie nostrae mentis, in qua scilicet resplendet imago beatissimae Trinitatis' (*Opera* V, 303).

his work'.[55] And just as St Bonaventure's 'Journey of the Mind towards God', the *Itinerarium mentis in Deum*, depends on the vivid awareness of one's own creaturely imperfection, so Descartes's journey retraces a closely similar path, intertwining philosophical argument with the awareness of our own finitude that has always formed a key element in the religious impulse. *Dubito, cupio* — in the very act of doubting, of desiring knowledge, I recognise my defects; and this would be impossible *si nulla idea entis perfectioris in me esset cujus comparatione defectus meos agnoscerem* ('if there were no idea of a more perfect being within me, by comparison with which I might recognise my defects').[56] Or as Bonaventure puts it, in phrasing so close to this that it is hard to believe Descartes was not directly influenced by it: *Quomodo sciret intellectus hoc esse ens defectivum et incompletum, si nulla haberet cognitionem entis absque omni defectu?* ('How would the intellect know that this was a defective and incomplete being, if it had no awareness of a being free from every defect?')[57]

But despite all the parallels, there is between classical or medieval thinking on the one hand and the early modern outlook on the other a great gulf fixed — a gulf shaped not so much by the enlarged scope of human knowledge as by the possibility of developing a radically new *kind* of knowledge, more active, more dynamic than anything that had gone before. In the post-Renaissance world, it was becoming clear for the first time just how searchingly the book of nature could be interrogated, and the relationship of humankind to creation was thereby subtly altered. The triumphant activism of the *Discourse* contains Descartes's best-known declaration of the change: we are to become 'maîtres et possesseurs de la nature'.[58] Just as striking is a crucial transition at the start of Part Three of the *Principles of Philosophy*, where we find encap-

---

[55] AT VII 51; CSM II 35. The Christianised Platonic language occurring in this part of the Third Meditation carries echoes that go back as early as St Basil: 'Since through an illuminating power we reach forth to the beauty of the Image of the Invisible God, and through that come to the surpassing vision of the Archetype, this cannot take place apart from the presence of the Spirit of knowledge, who gives . . . to those who love the vision of truth the power to behold the Image . . .' Basil, *On the Holy Spirit* [*De spiritu sancto*, c. 370], XXVIII 47 (ed. C. F. Johnston (Oxford: Clarendon Press, 1892), pp. 94–5).
[56] 'Qua ratione intelligerim me dubitare, me cupere . . .?' (AT VII 46; CSM II 31).
[57] *Itinerarium* III, 3 (*Opera* V, 202).
[58] *Discourse on Method*, part vi (AT VI 62; CSM I 142–3).

sulated, in the space of two paragraphs, the move from the contemplative to the active critical mode. Acknowledging God's handiwork in creation, Descartes observes, may lead to *Deum ob admiranda ejus opera suspiciendum* — adoring God for his marvellous works — but there immediately follows a description of the *usus phenomenorum sive experimentorum ad philosophandum*: it is to experiential phenomena that the philosopher must turn in order to explain and understand.[59]

This counterpoint between the contemplative and the controlling runs, in one way or another, through all or much of Descartes's work. If we are looking for symbols to sum up these two poles of Cartesian thinking, we might think respectively of the *sun* and the *stove*. On the one hand there is the Platonic image of the philosopher emerging to contemplate the sun, that is the Form of the Good, or in its Christian manifestation, the God who dwells in 'light inaccessible'.[60] This supreme perfection is an object of awe and worship, to be gazed on, as Descartes says, 'in so far as the eye of my darkened intellect can bear it'.[61] On the other side we have the image of Descartes's *poêle* — the stove that he used to keep warm during his troubled night of dreams in Bavaria where he had the vision of a new scientific system. No object of awe, but a mundane piece of machinery, put to use in the service of human convenience; this exactly corresponds to the physical universe as conceived of in Descartes's scientific manifesto — a lifeless series of mechanisms to be manipulated and controlled to our own advantage by the new *philosophie pratique*. Such a science, says Descartes, will enable us to understand and control all the objects in our environment as effectively as mechanics and artisans now manipulate their instruments, and so provide mankind with real power and control undreamt of by the contemplative and speculative philosophy of the past.[62]

---

[59] *Principia philosophiae* [1644], part II, arts. 3 & 4 (AT VIIIA 81; CSM I 249).
[60] 1 Timothy 6:16.
[61] Third Meditation, final paragraph (AT VII 52; CSM II 35).
[62] 'Au lieu de cette philosophie speculative qu'on enseigne dans les écoles, on en peut trouver une pratique, par laquelle, connaissant la force et les actions de . . . tous les . . . corps que nous environnent, aussi distinctement que nous connaissons les divers metiers de nos artisans, nous les pourrions employer en même façon, à tous les usages auxquels ils sont propres, et ainsi nous rendre comme maîtres et possesseurs de la nature' (AT VI 62; CSM I 142).

One might think that history has vindicated the controlling voice of Descartes at the expense of the contemplative. We do not get from nature the kind of knowledge that can be of direct practical use if we contemplate her beauty and wonder, but only if we analyse and measure and interrogate. That is the message of Descartes's manifesto of 1637, and it remains largely dominant today. Immanuel Kant famously identified the starry heavens above us as an enduring source of awe (*Achtung*), but it is striking that Descartes never once, to my knowledge, adopts the awestruck or contemplative mode when referring to any part of the physical universe.[63] As a schoolboy in the chapel at La Flèche he must many times have heard the psalm *Caeli enarrant gloriam Dei*,[64] but the only adoration found in his writings is that inspired by the results of the inward search for God within the recesses of his own mind.

The Moral Dimension: Manipulation or Meditation?

The sharp disparity between Descartes's metaphysical and his scientific *modus operandi*, the gulf between the contemplative and the controlling mindsets, seems to me to affect all parts of Cartesian philosophy; and it reappears prominently when we move to the moral branches of the system, which Descartes saw as bearing some of the principal fruits of his philosophy.[65] Here the tension emerges as a contrast between, on the one hand, a vision of the good life as a life of contemplative submission to the good (a kind of analogue of what theologians describe as openness

[63] Perhaps the nearest Descartes comes to this is in his account of the machinery of the body, where he comments on how far the ingenuity and intricacy of the divine craftsman exceeds that of the human artisan (*Discourse on Method*, part v, AT VI 55–6; CSM I 139). But the point of this passage is not to express awe at the handiwork of God for its own sake, but rather to reinforce the argument that, since we know ingenious automata can be constructed even by human hands, there is no bar in principle to explaining the automatic responses of human and animal bodies in just such purely mechanical terms.

[64] 'The Heavens declare the glory of God' (Psalm 19 (Authorised Version) or 18 in The Vulgate).

[65] Morals is one of the branches of the Cartesian tree of knowledge from which the fruit may be gathered: *Les Principes de la Philosophie, Lettre préface de l'édition Française* [1647], AT IXB 14; CSM I 186.

to divine grace), and, on the other hand, a more autonomous ideal of a life tailored to human needs and utilising the resources of the new science to control and modify the mechanisms of the body.

The older contemplative view that held sway in the centuries before Descartes is perhaps best exemplified by the Augustinian-inspired vision of Bonaventure; the model of divine illumination that we have seen as pervading Bonaventure's metaphysics is fully carried over into his moral philosophy. There is (as Etienne Gilson acutely observes in his study of Bonaventure) a divine illumination of the virtues corresponding to the divine illumination of our ways of knowing. For Bonaventure, the virtues are divinely imprinted marks left on the will to render it good, just as theoretical ideas are marks left on the intellect to make it capable of attaining truth: 'they are imprinted in the soul by the exemplary light and produce their effect in the realm of feeling and action, just as in cognition'.[66]

In his influential exposition of the virtues, St Ambrose, the bishop who had baptised Augustine in 387, isolated four as 'cardinal' — *prudentia, temperantia, constantia, justitia* (prudence or practical wisdom, temperance, firmness or fortitude, and justice);[67] the source for Ambrose was Cicero, whose typically derivative contribution in turn takes us directly back to Plato.[68] In the *Republic* Plato famously argues that on the individual level each human being, to lead a good and harmonious life, has to have a well-ordered soul; such an individual will be wise (with the wisdom of the rational element in control), courageous (with the 'spirited' element displaying bravery in the service of reason), temperate (with the desires properly subordinated to the rationally perceived good), and finally just (with each element working in harmony with the others).[69] Bonaventure, who will again serve as an apt spokesman for the tradition, summarises the widely accepted rationale for the cardinality thesis with tolerable accuracy when he observes that

---

[66] 'Haec imprimuntur in anima per illam lucem exemplarem et descendunt in cognitivam, in affectivam, in operativam.' Bonaventure, *In Hexaëmeron* [1273], VI 10 (*Opera* V 362). Cf. E. Gilson, *La Philosophie de Saint Bonaventure*, p. 423.

[67] Aquinas, *Summa theologiae* [1266–73], Ia IIae q61, 1–5. Cf. IIa IIae qq47–170.

[68] Cicero, *De finibus* [45 BC], V xxiii 67; Plato, *Republic*, 427e; *Laws* [c. 350 BC], I 631.

[69] *Republic*, 441–4.

temperance, practical wisdom, constancy and justice are called 'cardinal' for three possible reasons: 'because they are the gateway to the acquisition of all the virtues; or because it is chiefly in them that each virtue is made whole; or because through them every aspect of human life has to be directed and regulated.'[70]

Steeped as he was in the Augustinian–Platonic tradition, one might have expected Descartes to plug into the doctrine of the four cardinal virtues when he came to develop his own moral theory. Given that the *Passions of the Soul* has as one of its key objectives the unfolding of how we may achieve a good life through the mastery of the passions, it might seem that the traditional quartet would be a highly appealing apparatus. An imaginary Descartes, inspired in this way, might perhaps have presented us with a quadripartite vision of *wisdom* (derived from the clear and distinct ideas of metaphysics) running the show; *firmness* or *constancy* displayed in resolutely focusing on the truths so illuminated; *temperance* manifested in the resulting control of bodily desires to bring them into line with the perceived good; and finally *justice* (perhaps anticipating the later line of Spinoza) shown in the collective cooperation of free men individually guided by reason. But it was not to be. Instead, in the *Passions de l'âme*, we find no breath of a mention of the cardinal virtues; in ignoring them, Descartes might almost be writing under the aegis of Aristotle, whom Bonaventure bitterly criticises for his failure to grasp the importance of the cardinal quartet.[71] More alarming still to theological sensibilities, Descartes seems at times to have abandoned the very notion of the interiority of virtue, the Platonic intrapsychism that is so appealing to the Christian philosophers.

In many passages a far more dynamic or reactive conception of the good life emerges, premised partly on the idea of the value of training and habituation, found so prominently in Aristotle, but supplemented by

[70] 'Cardinales [sc. temperantia, prudentia, constantia, justitia] dicuntur tripliciter: vel quia per ipsas est ingressus ad acquirendum omnes virtutes; vel quia sunt principales in quibus integratur omnis virtus; vel quia omnis ratio vitae humanae habet dirigi et regulari per eas.' *In Hexaëmeron* VI 11 (*Opera* V, 362).

[71] *In Hexaëmeron* VI 11 (*Opera* V, 362): 'Aristoteles nihil de his sensit' ('Aristotle knows nothing of them'). For a different view, see D. S. Oderberg, 'On the Cardinality of the Cardinal Virtues', *International Journal of Philosophical Studies*, 7 (3) (1999), 305–22.

a highly ambitious and radically new conception of what falls within the scope of such training. The key to this radical activism is Descartes's vision of how the results of physiological science could be harnessed to the service of ethics. He wrote to a correspondent in 1646 that his results in physics had been 'a great help in establishing sure foundations in moral philosophy';[72] and when he published his treatise on the *Passions* in 1649 he distinguished his approach from that of many of his predecessors by stressing his goal of explaining the passions *en physicien* — from the point of view of a physical scientist.[73] What Descartes has in mind here is a systematic programme for the retraining of our psychophysical responses. The details of this programme[74] are based partly on his observations of how the behaviour of animals can be modified by appropriate conditioning; partly on observations in his own case of how various patterns of emotional response can be triggered by an arbitrary physical stimulus previously associated with a certain outcome (a striking example is his description of how he freed himself from a tendency to be attracted to cross-eyed women, a conditioned erotic response caused by a forgotten childhood infatuation with a girl with a squint); and partly by his general investigations of the psycho-physiology of the affective system.[75]

Descartes's activist dream that human beings should become masters and possessors of nature thus now encompasses human nature as well. Scientific mastery will extend not only to the natural environment, but also to the mechanisms of our own bodies (indeed, the material structure and the laws of operation are no different inside the body from what they are outside). And since the bodily events are inextricably linked to affective events (the passions of the soul), and since virtue is about a life of harmony between reason and the passions, science opens the door to a

[72] 'la notion telle quelle de la Physique, que j'ai tâché d'acquérir, m'a grandement servi pour établir des fondements certains en la Morale' (letter to Chanut of 15 June 1646, AT IV 441; CSMK 289).
[73] AT XI 326; CSM I 327.
[74] Examined at length in J. Cottingham, *Philosophy and the Good Life* (Cambridge: Cambridge University Press, 1998), ch. 3.
[75] *Ibid*. For animal training, cf. *Passions of the Soul*, art. 50; for the girl with a squint, cf. Letter to Chanut of 6 June 1647 (AT V 57; CSMK 323).

practical recipe for virtue. Habituation, as Aristotle foresaw, will be the
key; but it will no longer rely on the luck of having a certain kind of
childhood training, since it is now in our power to reprogramme ourselves, armed with scientific knowledge of how our psycho-physical
responses operate. 'Even those whose souls are most feeble would be
able to gain an absolute mastery over all the passions, if enough effort
were devoted to training and guiding them (*à les dresser et à les
conduire*).'⁷⁶ The 'dressage' envisaged here, at the end of Part One of the
Passions of the Soul, is aimed at nothing less than adjusting the pattern
of brain movements (*les mouvements du cerveau*) and their associated
feelings — a systematic reprogramming of our inherited and acquired
psycho-cerebral responses.

This in turn opens up enormous scope for autonomous human action,
in contrast to the essential quietism of the Platonic- and Stoic-inspired
conceptions of moral philosophy that had formed much of the background to previous moral thinking. The quietist analysis of the human
condition had rested on two pillars: the unalterability of the natural
environment, and the danger posed by the passions to our tranquillity.
And the cure was to accept with resignation the externals that we cannot
change, and to cleanse our internal life of recalcitrant passion so that
it can no longer lead us astray.⁷⁷ In Descartes's moral philosophy, by
contrast, the externals no longer have to be taken as givens, since the
power of science can control and modify them; and the passions no
longer have to be feared or shunned, since they can be managed and
redirected, so as to provide, without threat to our pursuit of the good,
the pleasures they are naturally fitted to provide — the 'greatest sweet-

⁷⁶ 'Ceux mêmes qui ont les plus faibles âmes pourraient acquérir un empire très absolu
sur toutes les passions, si on employait assez d'industrie à les dresser et à les conduire'.
Passions of the Soul, art. 50.
⁷⁷ For the standard Stoic recipe for the control of the passions, see J. Cottingham,
Philosophy and the Good Life, ch. 2, §4 (where some alternative interpretations of the
Stoic view of the passions are referred to). The question of Plato's attitude to the passions
is an immensely vexed one, and I am well aware that to group the 'Platonic' and 'Stoic'
approaches under the same broad heading is to ignore many complexities, particularly in
Plato's writings on the passions and the good life. For some of the complexities, see for
example Martha Nussbaum, *The Fragility of Goodness* (Cambridge: Cambridge
University Press, 1986), chs. 5–7.

ness that life has to offer (*le plus de douceur en cette vie*)'.[78] This optimistic vision of the ethical future for mankind here in the concluding article of the *Passions of the Soul* is strikingly prefigured in a letter written a few months earlier, where Descartes vividly distances himself from the old strategy of suppression: *La philosophie que je cultive n'est pas si barbare ni si farouche qu'elle rejette l'usage des passions; au contraire, c'est en lui seul que je mets toute la douceur et la félicité de cette vie.*[79]

In a persuasive analysis of the young Descartes's night of troubled dreams in his 'stove-heated room', the great Cartesian scholar Geneviève Rodis-Lewis sees the much-discussed symbol of the melon as representing the forbidden fruit of the tree of knowledge: *ne s'agirait-il pas du péché suprême et originale: vouloir rivaliser avec Dieu?*[80] The new Cartesian ethic so far expounded does indeed seem to take us in that hubristic direction — towards the idea of a wholly autonomous human species, bringing under control all the recalcitrant externals that had hitherto threatened the search for fulfilment, and even modifying the conditions of its own affectivity by scientific manipulation.

But although this is a recurring theme in Cartesian ethics, it never completely swamps the older Platonic and Augustinian resonances that we have been hearing elsewhere in Descartes's system. The continued pull Descartes felt back towards the Augustinian fold is signalled with a flourish at the start of Part Three of the *Passions*: 'I observe but a single thing which could give us just cause to esteem ourselves, namely the use of our free will, and the dominion we have over our volitions' (art. 152). True virtue, Descartes proclaims in the following article, is a matter not of outward achievement but of the inner exercise of our will. 'Nothing truly belongs to us but the freedom to dispose our volitions, and we ought to be praised or blamed for no other reason than for using this freedom

---

[78] 'L'âme peut avoir ses plaisirs à part. Mais pour ceux qui lui sont communs avec le corps, ils dépendent entièrement des passions: en sorte que les hommes qu'elles peuvent le plus émouvoir sont capables de goûter le plus de douceur en cette vie' (*Passions of the Soul*, art. 212).

[79] Letter to Silhon of March or April 1648; AT V 135.

[80] G. Rodis-Lewis, *Descartes* (Paris: Calmann-Levy, 1995), p. 67. Cf. the letter she cites, of 1 February 1647 (AT IV 608–9; CSMK 309).

well or badly.'[81] And because it depends on such an inner resolve, rather than anything external, Descartes is able to add a universalist corollary that calls to mind his earlier allegiance in the *Discourse* to the Christian principle that salvation is open to all: those possessed of virtue so defined will rejoice in the 'virtuous will for which they alone esteem themselves, and which they suppose also to be present, or at least capable of being present, in every other person'.[82] The good life is not the autonomous power to re-create ourselves or the environment, but the use of our God-given free will to bring our lives into conformity with divinely generated truth and goodness.

Conclusion

There is no doubt a historical interest in mapping out classical and Christian strands in Descartes's philosophy, and comparing them with the revolutionary aspirations he has for his new scientific system. But if historians of philosophy are to be more than antiquarians, we must always ask what is the *philosophical* point of our enquiries. I do not mean by this that we should always try to force our historical materials through the fashionable mangle of 'up-to-date' analytic philosophy; for much modern work on ethics (in the Anglophone tradition at least) runs a serious risk of becoming obsessive and short-sighted as it scrutinises intricate conceptual puzzles in almost total abstraction from the cultural and philosophical tradition that delivered us where we are today. But equally, I would suggest that the history of philosophy can easily turn sterile if it lacks a sense of how the issues of the past are related to a continuing philosophical quest. Fruitful philosophical analysis, like individual self-discovery, operates at a point of interplay between the

---

[81] *Passions of the Soul*, art. 153 (AT XI 446; CSM I 384). The self-esteem of the Aristotelian *megalopsychos* was the satisfaction of one whose outward achievements match his sense of self-worth; the self-esteem enjoyed by the Cartesian *généreux* will depend on the 'firm and constant resolution to use our freedom well'.

[82] *Passions, of the Soul*, art. 154 (AT XI 446–7; CSM I 384; emphasis supplied). Compare *Discourse*, part I: 'the road to heaven is no less open to the most ignorant than to the most learned' (AT VI 8; CSM I 114).

struggle towards a future not yet achieved, and the effort to recover and understand the past we have (partly) left behind.[83]

What is at stake, then, philosophically, in the efforts of Descartes as a 'modern' moral philosopher to come to terms with the different strands from his Christian and Pagan antecedents? One of the main issues which I hope has emerged is the question of how far we can reconcile two distinct conceptions of how we should live — both in the practical sense of how we should conduct our daily lives, and also perhaps in the theoretical sense of how we should philosophise, how we should search for enlightenment. Should our posture be one of active, critical engagement with the conditions in which we find ourselves situated: should we be modifiers, changers, addressing ourselves to the world as would-be masters and possessors of our destiny? Or should we adopt the posture of submission and contemplation, rejecting the allure of control over externals as essentially irrelevant to the spiritual task of realising our true selves?

Put in this perhaps somewhat portentous way, the question tends to answer itself. One cannot, in philosophy, any more than in life, go backwards. The scientific revolution that Descartes and his contemporaries inaugurated has irreversibly changed the relationship of humankind to our environment: the conditions of nature, the structures of our own bodies, are, whether we like it or not, now within our direct power to alter in very substantial and significant ways. To go back to the quietist, contemplative strategy is, in an important sense, no longer an option.

Yet even if we accept the Cartesian apologia for modernity and the new scope science affords for ameliorating our lot, a crucial question remains about what constitutes the central core of the good life for humankind; and this is a question that is by no means settled by the increased power over externals that modern man now enjoys. Descartes himself would have been well versed in at least three kinds of approach to this core question that were prominent in the ancient world. For the epitome of Aristotelian virtue, the *megalopsychos* or 'great-souled man',

[83] I take this point from my General Introduction to *Descartes' Meditations: Background Source Materials*, ed. R. Ariew, J. Cottingham and T. Sorell (Cambridge: Cambridge University Press, 1998).

self-fulfilment realistically involved external achievement, a comfortable degree of success in the 'great and celebrated undertakings'[84] that are the appropriate display of excellence of character. For the Stoics, reverting to a more austere conception partly inspired by Plato, fame, fortune and all such worldly perquisites of achievement are simply *adiaphora* — perhaps worth pursuing under certain circumstances, and so 'to be chosen' (*lepta*), but not to be valued in themselves.[85] Finally, and in the starkest contrast of all to the achievement-oriented stance of Aristotle, we have the message of the Gospels in the first century AD: worldly wealth and success are not merely morally irrelevant to the virtuous life, but are positive *obstacles* to blessedness. Those picked out by the beatitudes in the fifth chapter of Matthew are precisely those who, in virtue of the circumstances of their lives, are at farthest remove from the natural environment of the *megalopsychos*.

Compare now the final verdict reached by Descartes himself, when he reflects on the conditions for the good life and concludes that fulfilment lies not in the aggressive manipulation of the external conditions of our existence, but in the cultivation of moral integrity:

> Provided the soul always has the means of happiness within itself, all the troubles coming from elsewhere are powerless to harm it. If anyone lives in such a way that his conscience cannot reproach him for ever failing to do something he judges to be the best, he will receive from this a satisfaction that has such power to make him happy that the most violent assaults of the passions will never have sufficient power to disturb the tranquillity of his soul.[86]

[84] Aristotle, *Nicomachean Ethics* [*c*. 325 BCE], 1124b.

[85] For the Stoic distinction between *adiaphoron* ('indifferent') and *lepton* ('to be taken'), described in Diogenes Laertius and Stobaeus, see A. A. Long and D. N. Sedley (eds.), *The Hellenistic Philosophers* (Cambridge: Cambridge University Press, 1987), sect. 58.

[86] 'Pourvu que notre âme ait toujours de quoi se contenter en son intérieur, tous les troubles qui viennent d'ailleurs n'ont aucun pouvoir de lui nuire . . . Car quiconque a vécu en telle sorte que sa conscience ne lui peut reprocher qu'il n'ait jamais manqué à faire toutes les choses qu'il a jugées être les meilleures . . . il en reçoit une satisfaction qui est si puissante pour le rendre heureux, que les plus violents efforts des passions n'ont jamais assez de pouvoir pour troubler la tranquillité de son âme.' *Passions of the Soul*, art. 148. Despite the stress on *satisfaction* in this passage, it is in my view best construed *not* as asserting the shallow thesis that the value of virtue lies in the utility payoff for the practitioner, but simply as making the important and encouraging observation that the

The resounding conclusion reached here is reinforced by Descartes's final definition of virtue, a few paragraphs later, as a 'firm and constant resolution to use our freedom well, that is, never to lack the will to undertake and carry out what we judge to be best'.[87] In this sense, virtue is self-validating, because it gives us the way to be what we were meant to be, or what we can best become: human beings who fulfil our capacities for goodness, love, courage, generosity and the like. And those capacities are realised in the moral character of the lives we can choose to lead, not principally by the degree of power we have over our bodies or their environment.

In the conclusions reached in his last published work, Descartes in the end moves the emphasis away from the ambition of command and control, and turns back to a distillation of what is best and deepest in Platonic, Stoic and Christian thought — that the only thing that ultimately matters in our lives is the inner character of our response to goodness.[88] It is no accident that in this idea of subordinating our resolve so as to execute what we judge to be best, we are taken back to the theme of the divine light so prominent in Descartes's metaphysics. Deeply embedded in Descartes's philosophy is the idea that the good, once clearly perceived, compels our allegiance, just as the truth compels our assent. The human ethical journey consists in training ourselves to have the resolve to continue on the right way, even though (because of the

---

virtuous life does indeed offer benefits for the agent. To make such an observation as part of the advocacy of the life of virtue is in fact quite compatible with allegiance to the more profound Stoic and Christian insight that virtue is valuable for its own sake — that, to use Kantian language, it shines like a jewel in its own right, irrespective of external accolades or even an internal psychic glow.

[87] *Passions of the Soul*, art. 153, speaking of the master virtue of 'generosity'.

[88] One might suppose that there is no irresolvable tension in the final position Descartes reaches here; for it could plausibly be argued that the mechanical manipulations of the scientist in modifying our psycho-physiology can be put to the service of the intellectual vision of the good: the ideal state for humans is when the passions are 'adjusted' so as to pull us in what our judgement independently perceives to be the right direction. Nevertheless the 'new-scientific' and the 'Platonic' strategies for ethics are logically distinct: the first envisages a bypassing of the need for temperance, through radical reprogramming of the passions; the second involves the more traditional model of gazing upon the good and exercising temperance so as to act in accordance with it.

inherent weakness of the human mind) we cannot always be attending to the 'immense light' that shows us which direction to take. Here the Platonic motif he inherited from Augustine and Bonaventure exactly subserves for Descartes, as it did for his medieval predecessors, the faith he shared with them. The initial impetus and the final goal of the quest for virtue is the immense light of truth and goodness, the source of every good and every perfect gift.[89,90]

---

[89] Bonaventure invokes at the very start of his own metaphysical journey 'the first principle from whom all lights descend, the Father of lights [*Pater luminum*], who is the source of *every good and every perfect gift*'. The phrase recapitulates the Epistle General of James [*c*. AD 50], 1:17: *pasa dosis agathe kai pan dôrema teleion anôthen esti, katabainon apo tou patros tôn phôtôn* ('Every good and every perfect gift is from above, coming down from the father of lights').

[90] I am most grateful to Michael Ayers for helpful comments on the penultimate draft of this paper.

3

Comments on Cottingham
'Plato's Sun and Descartes's Stove'

DOUGLAS HEDLEY

JOHN COTTINGHAM PRESENTS instances of Descartes's 'Platonism' in his cosmology, metaphysics and ethics. It is perhaps instructive to consider the extent to which the avowed Platonists of the period, such as Henry More (1614–87) and Ralph Cudworth (1617–88), differ from Descartes. I will concentrate less upon the direct legacy of Plato's dialogues than upon Platonism as a force within Descartes's milieu.

The major strand of Platonism up to the early nineteenth century was the Florentine Christian Neoplatonic synthesis, evident in the Cambridge Platonists, and still, even if much modified, in Hegel and Schelling. The 'Platonism' of Descartes is clearly different, much less consciously appropriated, and much more part of the unconscious Platonism of his milieu. As Cottingham implicitly acknowledges, Descartes's 'Platonism' — like that of Bonaventura (1221–74) — is more or less unconscious in contrast to the self-conscious and avowedly Platonising synthesis of the great Florentine humanist, Marsilio Ficino (1433–99). Descartes's Platonism is largely derived from Augustine and is accepted as part of a *Christian Weltanschauung* rather than as a set of philosophical principles and arguments. Such Platonism might be called *implicit* Platonism, the (Neo)platonism of Ficino or Cudworth *explicit* Platonism, by which I mean the professed adherence to Platonism as a school of thought. Henry More is happy to see convergence here. He declares that he takes a more traditional Platonic path than Descartes, but that they start from the same point and reach the same goal:

Proceedings of the British Academy, **149**, 45–51. © The British Academy 2007.

we both setting out from the same Lists, though taking several ways, the one travelling in the lower Road of Democritism, *amidst the thick dust of Atoms and flying particles of* Matter; *the other tracing it o'er the high and aiery Hills of Platonism, in that more thin and subtil Region of* Immateriality, meet together notwithstanding at last (and certainly not without a Providence) *at the same Gaol* [sic], namely at the Entrance of the holy Bible . . .[1]

There is much in More's philosophical poems that expands this view,[2] and indeed in the nineteenth century S. T. Coleridge spoke of More as one of the 'Cartesian Platonists'.[3] One significant difference between Descartes and most Platonists, however, is in their method. Most of the Platonists see philosophy as *commentary* on ancient and received wisdom, and this is clearly very different from the Cartesian (and self-consciously modern) project of a philosophical *tabula rasa*.

Cosmology

Cottingham emphasises the congruence between the *Timaeus* of Plato and Descartes's cosmology. Descartes just assumes the Middle Platonic–Augustinian doctrine of the Platonic ideas as contained *within* the divine intellect. The relation of this position to Plato's own views is impossible to decide — even in so far as we may legitimately surmise what Plato's own position was, expressed as it is in dialogue or even myth within dialogue. Most patristic and medieval Christian writers did not worry about Aristotle's 'third man argument' or Plato's own reaction to that critique, but used Platonic ideas that had already been 'baptised' in Christian theology, often in ignorance of their pagan source. Descartes is just following this common and Christianised tradition of Platonism.[4]

Cottingham notes, however, that 'the gap between acknowledging an inscrutable divine fiat and simply accepting the unexplained explanatory

[1] Henry More, *Philosophical Works* (London, 1712), p. XI.
[2] H. More, *A Platonick Song of the Soul*, ed. A. Jacob (Lewisburg, PA: Bucknell, 1998).
[3] S. T. Coleridge, *Collected Notes* IV (London: Routledge, 1990), 5079, Dec. 1823.
[4] A. H. Armstrong and R. A. Markus, *Christian Faith and Greek Philosophy* (London: Darton, Longman and Todd, 1960), pp. 16ff.

postulates of modern secular physics seems to be wafer thin' (p. 27), and such voluntarism provoked Cudworth's ire. Nevertheless, I think there is a difference between Hume and Descartes in that Hume shows just how hard it is for a *really* rigorous empiricist, one who assumes that knowledge is constituted exclusively by the 'experimental' methodology, to give an adequate account of science. This is because science, like everyday life, presupposes many convictions and principles that cannot be easily verified. Descartes's theology gives him better grounds for the acceptance of the coherence of nature in his cosmology than Hume's agnosticism can concede. The view that God could not deceive is a striking instance of how Descartes's theology (especially as it follows from God's infinite goodness) gives him some rationale for accepting the coherence of nature.

Cottingham must be right, however, about the general upshot of Descartes's philosophy. The Cartesian stripping nature of *value* provoked a Platonic counter-reaction up until the nineteenth century. For example, Kant's *Critique of Judgement* (1790) is a fascinating product of a broadly Platonising reaction to Descartes's mechanical natural philosophy and cosmology. Evincing the profound influence of Leibniz and the 'British Plato', Shaftesbury (and hence, indirectly, of the Cambridge Platonists), upon Kant, the ideas of beauty and purpose become, for the sage of Königsberg, the means by which we can appreciate (if only symbolically or non-conceptually) how nature and morality cohere in a purposive and ultimately providential universe. The Third *Critique* mediates between apparently incompatible realms, the phenomenal and the noumenal — between nature and freedom, the domains of the First and Second *Critiques* respectively.

Metaphysics

The intimate link between Descartes's Cogito and his proof of God's existence is clearly part of a pervasive Platonic theocentrism in seventeenth-century thought in which knowledge of God is the basis of all other knowledge. The Second Meditation leads on to the Third Meditation because the certainty of the self's knowledge of itself as a

finite and imperfect being points in turn to the infinite and perfect mind
of God. Finite subjectivity leads to the divine subject. The temporal
priority of the Cogito can mask the logical priority of the certainty of
divine existence articulated by the ontological argument. And it is
curious that, contrary to the widespread image of Descartes as the
harbinger of modern 'subjectivity' (a view of him advanced by Hegel and
Heidegger, for example), the theories of such Cartesians as Malebranche
and Spinoza are distinctly *theocentric*, tending to submerge the human
subject into God.

Ethics

Cottingham reflects upon the striking fact of the 'interiority of virtue'
(p. 36) for Descartes as a residual Platonic resonance in his ethics: 'True
virtue . . . is a matter not of outward achievement but of the inner exercise of our will' (p. 39). The typical approach to the virtues among the
Platonists is deeply ascetic, and one of the most illuminating aspects of
Cottingham's paper is his surprisingly strong assimilation of Descartes's
views and the austere Platonic/Stoic/Christian tradition of ethical ideals
in opposition to the worldly 'achievement-oriented stance' of Aristotle
and his 'great-souled' man (pp. 41–2). One is tempted to reflect upon the
implications of this observation for the much-discussed renewal of
'virtue ethics' by such contemporary thinkers as Anscombe and
MacIntyre. Cottingham's construal of Descartes's ethics as in some vital
respects counter-Aristotelian has an obvious kinship with Kant's radical
dislocation of moral self and worldly achievement.

Contemplation or Control?

The question of the complex ethical relationship between self and world
in Cottingham's admirably nuanced account of Descartes's thought
culminates in the question: 'Should our posture be one of active, critical
engagement with the conditions in which we find ourselves situated:
should we be modifiers, changers, addressing ourselves to the world as

would-be masters and possessors of our destiny? Or should we adopt the posture of submission and contemplation, rejecting the allure of control over externals as essentially irrelevant to the spiritual task of realising our true selves?' (p. 41).

Let me concede at once the persuasive force of Cottingham's analysis of the opposing tendencies in Descartes's thought. Moreover there is no doubt that Descartes's emphasis upon method is typical of the 'modern' tendency in seventeenth-century philosophy. Yet the thrust of Cottingham's reflections is philosophical rather than historical or sociological; and at such a philosophical level a Platonist may happily accept that contemplation and control may be fruitfully linked. Whereas Cottingham seems to suggest that both are inherently in direct opposition (for example, 'critical scrutiny' is opposed to 'humble submission' on p. 31), we do not need to construe the Platonic tradition as necessarily committed to such a strict alternative. The issue is less 'either or' than 'both and'. There are historically influential Platonists for whom control of nature can be seen as a benign by-product of contemplation. Indeed, Descartes's own image of philosophy as a tree with metaphysical roots and more practical branches in the other sciences suggests that the contemplative core of the subject is compatible with branches that offer immediate fruits.

Cottingham identifies contemplation with 'quietism'. And yet many of the great advances in the astronomy of early modern science were the result of a Platonic contemplative ideal, in which mathematics was of central importance. And in more modern science one can take the example of purely contemplative–theoretical discoveries that could then in turn be exploited in great technical innovations with enormous practical consequences. Electromagnetism and the telephone might be an example of this: the theoretical knowledge of electromagnetism *preceded* any perceived need to communicate across vast distances. The telegram and telephone were developed as products of the practical employment of the fruits of theoretical enquiry.[5] T. S. Eliot in 'Little Gidding' provides a fine account of the difference between contemplative *detachment* and *indifference*.[6] I think there is an analogy with

[5] A. E. Taylor, *Does God Exist?* (London: Collins, 1966), p. 78.
[6] T. S. Eliot, *Collected Poems* (London: Faber and Faber, 1974), p. 219.

science. The detached contemplation of truth does not imply an indifference regarding the fruits of discovery. But it does maintain that the goal
of science is not utility but truth. The Platonists proper are not averse to
action *per se*, but see action as derived from contemplation. The
theorems of Euclid and Pythagoras have, in fact, changed the world;
though they do not, I think, look like practical discoveries.[7] Plotinus likes
to express this idea by saying that 'Action is a weakening of contemplation' (*Ennead* III viii 4).

A pertinent illustration of contemplative control outside the bounds
of strict science can be found in S. T. Coleridge's fine depiction of
Shakespeare's genius as that of one who 'first studied patiently, medi-
tated deeply, understood minutely, till knowledge become habitual and
intuitive, wedded itself to his habitual feelings, and at length gave birth
to that stupendous power, by which he stands alone, . . .'[8] And perhaps,
one might suggest, inner vision is more important for the intelligent and
sensitive transformation of the world than any merely mechanical
modification of the external environment. One might think of the enormous *practical* effect of such visionary prophets as Moses or
Mohammed, or contemplative philosophers such as Socrates or Hegel, to
say nothing of Wilberforce or Gandhi, upon world affairs. Mahatma
Gandhi is a striking instance. His asceticism and his political engagement
were closely linked to his adherence to the great monistic Vedantic metaphysics of Sankara (eighth century AD). And the frequently serendipitous
relationship between discovered fact and the formation of hypotheses can
be observed in such figures as Newton and Einstein. Both were men of
great imagination and neither lacked a contemplative sensibility. The
stories of Newton's apple and of Einstein brooding over the town clock
in Bern may be apocryphal, but they nicely illustrate the complex relationship between control of the world and contemplation of its nature.

[7] Michael Ayers has pointed out to me that Euclid may have been developing and systematising a more practical mathematics, but a Platonist would doubtless judge Euclid's
achievement as the fruit of contemplation. The fact that Proclus models his *Elements of
Theology* upon Euclid reflects a well-established Platonic esteem for mathematics as a
contemplative science. I think it no accident that Kepler praises 'Proclus the Platonic
Philosopher' in his *Harmonies of the World*.
[8] S. T. Coleridge, *Biographia Literaria* (Princeton, NJ: Bollingen, 1983), II 27.

In conclusion, one might argue that Platonism (whether implicit or explicit) is not quite as quietist as Cottingham implies. Of course 'control' has pejorative associations. But in fact the general optimism of *maîtres et possesseurs de la nature* has a certain (and perhaps surprisingly) Platonic origin. Plato's attack on the arts is closely linked to his rejection of the pessimistic anthropology of the tragedians. Hence, while for the tragedians 'Know thyself!' means 'Know thy limits and don't upset the gods!', Plato takes the Delphic imperative to mean 'Know the rational divine within!'[9] Like the Greek tragedians, the later Augustine has a gloomy view of human possibilities, but this is not the only Christian reception of the Platonic inheritance. Kepler and Ficino are striking instances of a Platonic optimism that extends beyond the Renaissance into the Enlightenment and beyond. Giovanni Pico della Mirandola's famous *Oratio* of 1486 pursues emphatically the idea of the intellectual dignity of mankind which is part of his curiously Platonic blend of hubris and piety. The Cambridge Platonists attack the determinism of Hobbes on the basis of a much more optimistic anthropology of clearly Platonic hue. Perhaps even Descartes's optimistic interest in the use of reason has a component of genuinely Platonic provenance. After all, Plato's zeal in establishing a utopian community is one of the most notorious aspects of his model of the philosopher's return to the cave.[10]

---

[9] Plato, *Alcibiades* I 133c 4–6. Cf. Aristotle, *Nichomachean Ethics* X 7; 1177b 30–34. I shall leave aside questions about the authenticity of the Plato passage or dialogue since my major concern is Plato's legacy.

[10] I am grateful to James Vigus and David Leech for comments and suggestions.

4

Spinoza, Platonism and Naturalism

MICHAEL AYERS

ANY GREAT PHILOSOPHICAL TEXT from the past invites the question, often rather urgently, of how such a thing came to be written. It will do so, at any rate, for the reader who reasonably hopes that knowledge of the context of its writing will resolve at least some, if not all, of the obscurity and ambivalence that inevitably attends a first reading. In the case of Spinoza's metaphysics, however, the uncertainties seem particularly resistant to contextual resolution. For there are at least three apparently very different ways of reading *Ethics* that can each draw justification not simply from some ingenious, uninformed interpretation of the words on the page, but from those words interpreted with a close eye on particular elements in the historical context of Spinoza's thinking.

Two Views of Spinoza

One approach, not now much in fashion, is epitomised in the work of Leon Roth[1] and Harry Austryn Wolfson.[2] Wolfson took Spinoza to be primarily a philosopher in the Jewish tradition, if an unorthodox and innovative one, engaged in debate with medieval, mainly Jewish, philosophers and their later followers in their own terms. Roughly, the first two books of *Ethics* were read as if Spinoza's main aim, however the pursuit of that aim may have been guided by acquaintance with the

[1] *Spinoza* (London: E. Benn, 1929).
[2] *The Philosophy of Spinoza: Unfolding the Latent Processes of his Reasoning* (Cambridge, MA: Harvard University Press, 1934). Wolfson assigns 618 pages to parts I and II, 50 to the other parts of *Ethics*, and 25 to conclusions.

Proceedings of the British Academy, **149**, 53–78. © The British Academy 2007.

philosophy of Descartes, was to purge Jewish philosophical and theological thought of error precisely by a more rigorous, critical and selective understanding and application of its own principles. The greatest single influence on Spinoza, both as teacher and as target, is taken to be Maimonides. Deep knowledge of this tradition, Wolfson supposed, was acquired by the young Spinoza before his expulsion from the Jewish religious community. An analysis of Spinoza's arguments directed by an understanding of this context, Wolfson thought, would show that behind his definitions, axioms and propositions there lurks a mind 'crammed with traditional philosophic lore', whose 'thought turns along the beaten logical paths of medieval reasoning'. This is 'the implicit Spinoza, . . . only occasionally revealing himself in the scholia'.[3] Virtually every assertion and argument in the first parts of *Ethics* stimulated Wolfson to find in the medieval, usually Jewish, tradition something either similar or contrary to it, on the assumption that it was that traditional thesis or reasoning that Spinoza was intending to adopt, transform or confront in the course of constructing his system.

To give just one example, Wolfson proposed that the six opening propositions of *Ethics*, in which it is argued that there can be no more than one substance of any given kind and that one substance cannot be produced by another substance, are directed against very specific medieval views about the emanation of creatures from God, such as the Neoplatonic doctrine of the emanation of a first intelligence.[4] Yet the argument in Part I, Propositions 1–6, is apparently about whatever is a substance, rather than about God in particular. Indeed, Proposition 5 appears to state that in the order of nature (*in natura rerum*) there cannot be two substances with the same attribute, and the expression '*in natura rerum*' is repeated not only in the Demonstration of this Proposition, but also in the Demonstration of Proposition 6, that one substance cannot be produced by another substance. Propositions 7 and 8, on the other hand, are to the effect, respectively, that any substance necessarily exists and that every substance is necessarily infinite. Only then need it dawn even on a careful, if unprimed, reader that the argument is narrowing the

---

[3] *Ibid.*, vol. I, p. vii.
[4] *Ibid.*, vol. I, ch. iv, esp. pp. 88–95.

substantial down to God (who is not explicitly mentioned until Proposition 11), rather than being concerned with natural substances as opposed to divine substance. The title of Part I, '*De Deo*', is hardly enough to warn the unsuspecting reader that Proposition 6 is the denial that God could create a substance — in effect, a denial of the very possibility of creation — rather than the more commonplace thought that one natural substance cannot create another (creation being the prerogative of God, who is above nature). Moreover, the argument is conducted in the terms of the Cartesian schema of substance, attribute and mode, and hinges on the issue of individuation. It therefore reads naturally (at least, until Propositions 7 and 8) as a critique of the multiplicity of Descartes's particular or individual substances, whether thinking or extended.[5] It would seem an odd way for Spinoza to set about refuting medieval doctrine to take the trouble to appear by his language to be engaging with Descartes, a cutting-edge philosopher to the exposition of whose theory Spinoza owed his public reputation as a metaphysician. In *The Principles of Descartes's Philosophy*,[6] the only work on metaphysics that Spinoza published in his lifetime, he had made it clear that he disagreed with at least some of the doctrines that he had very accurately expounded.[7] Its readers might naturally have expected Spinoza's *magnum opus* to set out the points of his disagreement, and it is an expectation that, in its opening paragraphs, *Ethics* seems well set to fulfil.

A second, long-standing and recently dominant approach to the interpretation of the first books of *Ethics* is more sensitive to the evidence that

---

[5] Even P7 and P8 *could* be read as (unorthodox) principles relating to matter and spirit, without identifying them with God. On the much-discussed question whether Descartes held that there is a multiplicity of particular extended substances or just one, see below.
[6] *Renati des Cartes principiorum philosophiae . . . (etc)* (Amsterdam, 1646).
[7] Good illustrations of his accuracy and understanding are supplied by his treatment of the relation between the two parts of Descartes's argument for mind–body dualism in the Second and Sixth Meditations, and by his exposition of Descartes's response to the charge that his argument validating clear and distinct perception is circular. Spinoza's self-conscious extension or strengthening of the latter argument is an illustration of his sympathetic resourcefulness in making Descartes's position an intelligible option. His view of these two elements of Descartes's argument is superior to much that has been written on them in recent decades. At the same time he allowed his disagreement with Descartes to show, although some of the signs may be easier to see with hindsight than they were for his first readers.

Descartes was, after all, a (or *the*) decisive influence on Spinoza's meta-physics. Recent work by Wiep van Bunge,[8] for example, takes the line that, so far from being the difficult child of the Jewish philosophical tradition, soaked in medieval lore, Spinoza was a quintessentially mid-seventeenth-century *Dutch* philosopher, whose own thought was formed precisely at a time when there was the greatest interest among Dutch intellectuals in Cartesian metaphysics and physics, as well as in the materialism, political philosophy and the philosophy of religion of Hobbes. Van Bunge argues that Spinoza showed only limited interest in Jewish thought after his early excommunication, the grounds of which are unknown. He points out that most of Spinoza's close associates were Christian Dutch supporters of republicanism. The concerns and debates of that community, van Bunge proposes, were what gave inspiration and purpose to Spinoza's thinking, while the quasi-geometrical form of *Ethics* itself, he thinks, reflects the intense interest in seventeenth-century Holland in the applications of mathematics. It had, after all, been in Holland, during his association with Isaac Beeckman, that Descartes's own interest in the possibilities of a mathematical or quantitative physics had been aroused.

Of these two views as to the context that stimulated and imbued Spinoza's metaphysics, it would seem to be the second, in so far as it involves close comparison with the philosophy of Descartes, that has proved the more illuminating. Nevertheless there are grounds for bring-ing the two views nearer together, grounds that relate to the topic of this paper, Spinoza and Platonism. Van Bunge notes that a section of Spinoza's early *Short Treatise on God, Man and his Well-being* owes something to a Jewish Platonist, Leon Ebreo, but he adds that 'all major commentators agree that the Platonic tendencies of the young Spinoza have been firmly eradicated from the mature philosopher's writings.' According to van Bunge, 'Spinoza was no Platonist.' Since Maimonides and other medieval and sixteenth-century Jewish philosophers were also

---

[8] E.g., in *From Stevin to Spinoza: an essay on philosophy in the seventeenth-century Dutch Republic* (Leiden: Brill, 2001). The quotations below are from 'The Use of Context: The early Enlightenment in the Dutch Republic', as delivered to a symposium on 'The new historiography of early modern philosophy', at the Warburg Institute, London, in November 2000.

deeply influenced by Platonic and, if that is different, Neoplatonic theory, it may seem important to the thesis that Spinoza was a quintessentially Dutch, rather than Jewish, philosopher that apparently Platonic elements in his mature thought are only apparently so. But is it really so important?

Early Modern Platonism and Descartes

One reason to allow that Spinoza, as a metaphysician, was primarily both stimulated by, and responding to, Cartesian theory and yet also significantly influenced by Platonic doctrine is that Descartes's metaphysics was itself largely shaped by Platonic notions. In effect, Descartes's physics was thereby given theological respectability by an implicit appeal to the authority of the greatest Christian Platonist, St Augustine. This affinity, the topic of John Cottingham's paper in the present volume (Chapter 2), is also brought centre-stage in a stimulating book by Thomas Lennon, *The Battle of the Gods and the Giants*,[9] the title of which is taken from Plato's characterisation of the dispute between 'lovers of the Forms' and empiricist–materialists. Lennon sees Descartes as chief of the former, with Gassendi as his primary opponent in the seventeenth-century version of the ancient conflict.[10]

Another stimulating book, *The Mind of God and the Works of Man*,[11] by Edward Craig, presents things rather differently. Craig sees the history of philosophy in terms of the rise and fall of different 'dominant philosophies', by which he means not worked-out philosophical systems, but guiding ideas that are generally accepted, even unquestioned for a time, within a particular culture. Such a guiding idea, according to Craig, typically arises outside systematic philosophy and has a pervasive influence beyond it, but will have deep and recognisable effects on the character of mainstream philosophy. The dominant such 'philosophical' idea of the seventeenth century, Craig argues, lay in the thought that man was made in the image of God. This ancient item in the Judaeo-Christian

---

[9] Princeton, NJ: Princeton University Press, 1993.

[10] See the Introduction to the present volume (Chapter 1) for discussion of this division.

[11] Oxford: Oxford University Press, 1987.

revelation was given new life at that particular time by being accorded an epistemological interpretation inspired, Craig reasonably asserts, by the progress of mathematical sciences. In certain respects, human beings are or can become like God, namely in the exercise of reason and the understanding of necessary truth.[12]

Craig has no difficulty illustrating his thesis by reference to a number of seventeenth-century philosophers, including Descartes, Spinoza and Leibniz. Yet what his argument boils down to is the selection of just one element in the theology characteristic of Christian Platonism as if it were the driving force behind that type of philosophical theory in the seventeenth century. Recourse to the doctrine that God made man in his image was a fairly routine appeal to revealed theology in vindication of human rationality and, in particular, of the theory of innate concepts or principles.[13] The question of how this theological doctrine could so resonate with philosophical thinking in the seventeenth century reduces, in effect, to the question of why Platonic notions were popular at the time. A full answer to that wider question would be likely to be pretty complicated. It would include, no doubt, an account of the part played by Platonism in the Italian Renaissance, and would recognise Platonism's very much earlier and continuing role in mainstream theology.[14] Craig is surely right to the extent that, at least by the time of Galileo, Mersenne and Descartes, an important part of the answer lies with the capacity of Platonism, or a certain kind of Platonism, to explain and underwrite the value of mathematics in the interpretation of the book of nature. Yet to include in the explanation of the popularity of Platonism the fact that the twenty-seventh verse of Genesis had taken hold of the collective consciousness would be, I think, to suppose the tail to be wagging the dog.

---

[12] The 'Similarity Thesis', as Craig calls it, could also have an ethical dimension. For Descartes, at least, human beings come closest to God in the exercise of will, a faculty in a certain sense infinite as human understanding is not.

[13] A different, if related, model for intellectual knowledge, also with roots in Plato and Augustine, is that of direct illumination by God. Although alluded to approvingly in the Third Meditation, it was adopted by Malebranche as a distinct alternative to Descartes's innatism.

[14] And, as Sarah Hutton's response to this paper (Chapter 5) argues, it would need to say something about the relation of Platonism to ideas present in the Kabbala — not to speak of other mystical writings.

In any case, it is open to question whether Platonic rationalism really was for long, if ever, *the* dominant philosophy, rather than one of the dominant philosophies, during the seventeenth century, since it was never without its influential sceptical and empiricist critics.

I speak of 'a certain kind of Platonism' since there are, notoriously, several different Platos, or directions in which different parts or periods of Plato's philosophising could be, and were, developed — not to speak of indeterminacies in particular works. Ancient scepticism owed a lot to the early Socratic Plato, Stoics drew on Plato's ethical theory and psychology, while Neoplatonists emphasised the metaphysics and theology of the late dialogues, and brought in Aristotelian theory. Aristotle himself can be read either as subverting core Platonist doctrine from a broadly empiricist, materialist point of view, or as endeavouring to maintain what he supposed to be the deep truth of Platonism (that is to say, at least, a teleological science incorporating an intelligible hierarchy of universals and method of division) while conceding more than Plato does to the role of sense-experience and to the ontological status of the particular objects of experience.

Early modern philosophers were similarly diverse, and ambiguous, in their reception of Platonic philosophy. Montaigne, for example, who is firmly categorised by Richard Popkin and others as a follower of Sextus Empiricus, was certainly an admirer of both Sextus and the sceptical Socrates. Yet he was unlike both in subordinating his scepticism to a high metaphysical division between Being and Becoming, theologically interpreted. We are, he tells us in effect, inhabitants of the world of Becoming, where both the objects and the subjects of cognition are continuously in flux, so that no human cognition and, by the same token, no human virtue naturally enjoys the secure permanence of true knowledge and true virtue. The only cognitive contact finite beings can have with that which truly and permanently *is*, and accordingly the only truly dependable goodness they are capable of, is by the grace of faith. Our natural faculties are just not up to it. The model is broadly Platonic, with direct appeal to a mystical work of the Neoplatonist, Plutarch of Chaeronea, but the divine gift of faith has supplanted rational understanding as our means of access to Being, and as the only way of rising above the shifting sands of Becoming. Faith is the one form of secure cognition and the one foundation of true virtue that is available to us. It is also one rarely granted, as hard experience of people's actions soon confirms, not least the hideous crimes committed in the name of religion. The best we can do is to try to prepare ourselves to receive divine illumination.[15]

Descartes's philosophy lies at the opposite end of this particular dimension of early modern Platonism, as Pascal in effect complained. Reason's traditional subject-matter, comprising eternal truths and essences or 'true and immutable natures', has been restored to it. The absolute permanence and security assigned to rational knowledge by Plato and a broad tradition is achieved by the famous argument of the Third Meditation, an argument that lifts our eyes to the first principle of all being and all understanding, God himself, and that ends with conventional allusion to the analogy of the sun in Plato's *Republic*. The argument appeals to another favourite Platonic notion, that of a hierarchy or scale of being, with God at the top and no upward causal flow. Ultimately, everything flows downward from a perfect and omnipotent being. The principle of Cartesian physics, moreover, that the quantity of matter and of motion is constantly maintained by God in accordance with immutable laws, satisfies two conditions required of any account of the world by Plato himself: first, that such an account should recognise what is permanent in change, and, second, that it should explain how mind orders everything for the best. Admittedly, Descartes's conception of the best is somewhat austere. The laws are rationally ascertainable, given our innate ideas of God and of geometrically defined matter, just because they are the most economical possible, driven, in effect, by a principle of least change. Teleology may in a sense have been kicked out of Descartes's material world, but it remains, if only just, in his account of the relationship of the world to God. Moreover, for Descartes as for Plato in *Timaeus*, sensations and passions are consequent on the embodiment of an intrinsically rational soul. They are necessary for the embodied life, but in their tendency to impede the natural functioning of reason they are causes of error and sin.[16]

[15] Montaigne, *Essais*, 'Apologie de Raymond Sebond'. Sebond's natural theology is defended, not as a way to knowledge, but as a part of the preparation for the grace of faith.
[16] Cf. Descartes, *Conversation with Burman* (AT V 149–50; CSM III 336): 'in infancy the mind is so swamped inside the body that the only thoughts it has are those which result

It is easy to downplay Descartes's Platonism just because Platonic or Neoplatonic concepts and theory were incorporated in so much later philosophy, not least at times when the systems of Plato and Aristotle were supposed harmoniously compatible. Adoption of the notions of a scale of being and of archetypes in the divine intellect, both freely taken over by Aristotelian scholastics, is hardly by itself evidence of serious Platonism. The same goes for the notion that genuine or scientific knowledge possesses an absolute security from future falsification, a principle of Plato's that was also maintained by scholastics — not to mention that it had been more or less definitive of the conception of knowledge shared by both sides in the centuries-long debate between Stoics and Sceptics. Descartes's employment of these notions is therefore liable to be explained by his working within the conceptual space of a fundamentally Aristotelian scholasticism, and even to be attributed directly to his Jesuit education. Yet it is surely true that in Descartes's philosophy such notions together form part of a firmly and self-consciously Platonic nexus, the decisive strand of which lies at the core of his epistemology: his particular treatment of the triangular relationship between universal ideas, the particulars that instantiate those ideas and are objects of the senses, and human minds equipped to interpret the data of sense by reference to universal ideas. Descartes's treatment of this triangle lies squarely within the Christian Platonist tradition: God, at the apex, creates things in accordance with universal archetypes, and creates human souls equipped with conceptions matching those archetypes, including conceptions to be made explicit and functional by the prompting of sense-experience. Not all Platonism is innatist, and not all innatism is Platonist, but this particular form of innatism is surely at least broadly Platonist.[17]

---

from the way the body is affected . . . The body is always a hindrance to the mind in its thinking, and this was especially true in youth.' (For an explanation of references to the works of Descartes in this form, see Abbreviations, p. ix.)

[17] I would not for a moment deny that Descartes was also powerfully influenced by the Stoic–Sceptic debate. Not only is that debate replicated to a significant extent in his own debate with a postulated sceptic, but also his analysis of judgement owes more to Stoic theory than to either Platonism or scholasticism. If anything, the relation of his epistemology to Stoicism (a relation not exclusively of indebtedness) has been underestimated.

If Spinoza too is a Platonist, the question arises whether that is simply in so far as he keeps within the Cartesian conceptual framework, or whether, in his departures from Descartes's system, he draws significantly on elements of Platonism that Descartes ignores, rejects or underplays. Evidently the last is the case. In particular, Descartes's employment of the notion of a scale of reality or being is allusive and perfunctory rather than a worked-out element in his system. God is at the top, finite spirits come next, then bodies, and finally non-substances or modes. But his principle that the cause of anything (including the cause of any idea) must have as much 'formal' reality as the effect has formal or (if it is an idea) 'objective' reality is an idiosyncratic version of the traditional causal principle. It is relied on for the particular conclusion that finite minds cannot be the cause of their idea of a perfect being, but little more is said about the scale of being. There are no specific echoes of hierarchical orders of emanation, the progress of the Many from the One, a characteristically Neoplatonic theme drawn ultimately from Plato's *Parmenides*.

Even the metaphysical unity of the created world gets little direct attention from Descartes. His material world is in a way strongly unitary, in so far as Cartesian matter can be regarded as just one continuous individual substance in internal motion, governed by a harmonious system of law. Yet he lays notoriously little emphasis on its unity. For whatever reason, his mechanics is set out, quasi-demonstratively, on what is by his own lights the merely ideal, strictly impossible assumption of absolutely hard bodies moving in straight lines and colliding in separation from the rest of matter—in effect in the vacuum ruled out by Descartes's own principles. Particular bodies or quantities of matter, moreover, are offered without apology as paradigms of entities between which there are real distinctions.[18] There is just possibly a more recondite connection with this aspect of Platonism. Descartes's controversial thesis that the eternal truths are themselves created, whatever its actual motiva-

---

[18] *Principles of Philosophy* I, sect. 60 (AT VIIIA 28; CSM I 213): 'Strictly speaking, a *real* distinction exists only between two or more substances; . . . For example, . . . we can . . . be certain that, if [any extended or corporeal substance] exists, each and every part of it, as delimited by us in our thought, is really distinct from the other parts of the same substance.' It is easy to see grounds for dissatisfaction with this account.

tion (the subject of much ingenious argument and little certainty), had some sort of antecedent in Platonic theory in the doctrine that divine Intellect, containing the Forms, is the first emanation from the One (the doctrine that came to be interpreted by Trinitarians as delineating the relation between the Father and the Son). But emanation was not routinely equated with arbitrary creation (to say the least), and in any case Descartes's theory would have been a sad disappointment to those who regarded monism in some form as a central truth of Platonism.[19]

Spinoza's Monism: the Unfolding of Perfect Being

In contrast, Spinoza's account of the emanation of multiplicity from the perfection of the divine nature might appear, at least from a distance and certain angles, as just another Neoplatonic theology, conforming to type. That he rejects creation by a transcendent intelligence is no reason to exclude him from the Platonist tradition, despite the role of the Demiourgos in *Timaeus* and the general acceptance of creation by orthodox mono-theists. Maimonides himself purported to weigh the pros and cons, com-ing down judiciously in favour of creation as the best explanation of the existence of particular things.[20] Spinoza's denial of creation is certainly consonant with the rigorous pursuit of the idea of the unity of being, an idea that found expression in some seventeenth-century Platonism in the quasi-idealist assertion that none of the distinctions we make between things are real distinctions, that all distinctions are distinctions of reason.

Spinoza does not, I think, openly and explicitly go as far as that, but he may do so in effect. In response to Tschirnhaus, for example, in what is probably his last extant letter,[21] he distinguishes 'simple things', which are 'beings of reason' defined by a single attribute, from 'real beings', answering to a real definition that can supply a rich list of properties. The given example of a real being is God, defined as a being whose essence

[19] And see Cottingham's remarks above on the doctrine of the creation of the eternal truths, pp. 25–7.
[20] Cf. L. E. Goodman, 'Maimonides, Moses', *Routledge Encyclopaedia of Philosophy* (London: Routledge, 1998), vol. 6, pp. 44–5.
[21] Letter 83, 15 July 1676.

includes existence. And it seems that, for Spinoza, God is the *only* 'real being' in this sense. Certainly his thesis that God is the only substance and Descartes's account of what 'real distinctions' are together entail that God is the only really distinct being, the only being that is not a 'being of reason', conceptually individuated.[22] And in any case Spinoza presents the progression or emanation of singular things from the unitary first principle less as the production of a real multiplicity than as something like the flowing of properties from essence, the logical unfolding of the unitary nature of reality.

The hierarchical descent described in Spinoza's theory conforms at least in general structure to Platonist accounts. It is, I think, worth considering in some detail how this is so, since the point is not generally given recognition. The first steps from the perfection of the divine nature, *first* to an infinity of such attributes as extension and thought, *then* to (what commentators agree in calling) 'immediate infinite modes', and *then* to 'mediate infinite modes', are all in some sense at the universal level, although the distinction between universal and particular is from the start blurred, to put it mildly, by the ontological status of the substance whose essence includes existence (whose universal nature, that is to say, includes there being this and only this particular instantiation of that nature). Finally there is the step to finite particulars, the mysterious step that since Plato has invited explication in terms of creation, although others before Spinoza had declined the invitation. One striking difference, however, between Spinoza's account and (as far as I am aware) all previous and contemporary Platonism is that other Platonists, in one way or another, placed matter low on the scale of being, whether as pure potentiality, or as mere appearance, or, in the way of Descartes and the Cambridge Platonists, as an inferior kind of substance. Spinoza, on the other hand, places extension up there, on the same ontological level as thought. How significant that is with respect to the question of his Platonism I will shortly consider.

Nevertheless the descent from the attribute of *thought*, at least, traces

---

[22] In *Ethics* I the argument goes in the opposite direction. The impossibility of drawing other than modal distinctions between either spirits or bodies (i.e., of there being a real multiplicity of either), together with the thesis that whatever is a substance is infinite, is taken to entail that there is just one substance.

a path that is very comparable to mainstream Platonism or Neoplatonism. Below thought comes the immediate infinite mode described in a letter[23] as 'absolutely infinite intellect', which seems to be the property of God in so far as he is an infinite thinking thing, capable of thinking 'infinitely many things in infinitely many ways' (*Ethics* IIP1D). This move at least roughly accords with the traditional, Plotinean notion of the first emanation from the One, which is universal Intellect, containing the Forms. If we needed evidence that Spinoza recognised this relationship to previous Platonist theology, it comes in the *Short Treatise*, in which he was still prepared to talk of creation as well as, more generally, of production. Here, in what might appear as a somewhat startling allusion to the Trinity,[24] he says of 'intellect in the thinking thing' that it 'is a Son, product, or immediate creature of God, . . . created by him from all eternity. Its sole property is to understand everything clearly and distinctly at all times.'[25] In the beginning was the Word.

It might not be such a popular view among Christian Platonists, however, that right up there with the *logos* is eternal motion, another 'Son' of God, or rather the same one considered under the attribute of extension. For the immediate infinite mode falling under extension is Cartesian motion and rest. In Part II of *Ethics* Spinoza argues that every mode of thought is identical with some mode of extension, and vice versa (*Ethics* IIP7S). One and the same mode can be considered under the two different attributes. We may suppose that infinite modes, as well as finite modes, are related in just this way. For the one substance, considered under the attribute of extension, to be such as to be in infinite and eternal motion is the *same* as for it to be, considered under the attribute of thought, such as to have infinite and eternal understanding. So much is implicit in Spinoza's famous principle, 'The order and connection of ideas is the same as the order and connection of things' (*Ethics* IIP7). It is just what symmetry demands.

This identity of infinite modes, I take it, is also assumed in what Spinoza says about mediate infinite modes. An example of a mediate

---

[23] Letter 64, to Schuller, 29 July 1675. Schuller was conveying queries put by Tschirnhaus.

[24] But see Sarah Hutton's comment below, pp. 83–4.

[25] *Short Treatise on God, Man and his Wellbeing* I.ix.

infinite mode given in the same letter is what he calls '*facies totius universi*'. This is generally translated 'the face of the whole universe', although a less metaphorical translation than 'face' might be 'make-up' or 'configuration', the way the universe is. Spinoza refers his correspondent to a passage in *Ethics* (IIP13S, lemma 7) where it is argued that the continued mechanical interaction of the parts of any body, provided that they interact in a fixed manner or *ratio*, involves no change in the *form* of the body. The whole body thereby persists as the same unified individual. Simple individuals can compose more complex ones and, he says, 'if we proceed in this way to infinity, we shall easily see that the whole of nature is one individual, whose parts, that is, all bodies, vary in infinite ways, without any change of the whole individual'. The form of the universe, it seems, is the limiting, only perfect case of the law-governed dynamic relationship between the parts of any individual in virtue of which that individual can survive change, that is to say, motion. Accordingly the Cartesian laws of mechanics constitute, in their operation, the principle of the unity and continuity of the universe as a whole, determining it as a persisting individual conceived under the attribute of extension. It has been thought by some that by '*facies totius universi*' Spinoza meant just these laws, just this 'form'. But that interpretation, I would suggest, must be wrong. It rudely abolishes symmetry, dislocating the mediate infinite mode falling under extension from the mediate infinite mode falling under thought.

With respect to the latter Spinoza argues to the effect that, given that the immediate infinite mode is absolutely infinite intellect, it follows that God actually, and not merely potentially, understands everything possible, so that there also necessarily falls under the attribute of thought the mediate infinite mode which is *idea Dei*, meaning 'God's idea'.[26]

---

[26] That Spinoza nowhere explicitly states what the mediate infinite mode of thought is or discusses its relation to the immediate infinite mode, 'absolutely infinite intellect', together with commentators' uncertainty as to what exactly '*facies totius universi*' refers to, has tended to leave them feeling free to speculate. The present reading is in my view by far the most straightforward. It accords with Joachim's, later criticisms of which seem to me weak. See H. H. Joachim, *A Study of the* Ethics *of Spinoza* (Oxford: Oxford University Press, 1901), pp. 94–5, and compare G. H. R. Parkinson, *Spinoza's Theory of Knowledge* (Oxford: Oxford University Press, 1954), p. 116.

God's idea is also 'the idea of God' in that it is, Spinoza tells us, the idea of God's essence and everything that follows from it, in other words, the idea of everything that is or could be (*Ethics* IIP3S).[27] Now everything that is possible, in Spinoza's system, is also both actual and necessary. God's perfection entails, under the attribute of extension, not only the existence of motion and rest and the laws of motion and rest, but the precise ways in which the laws are instantiated. Not only the form but, as it were, the content of the universe, its actual configuration, is for Spinoza absolutely (and eternally) necessary. That has been denied by some commentators, but Spinoza's words are unequivocal, and his thought seems clear enough. He roundly asserts, for example, 'Things could have been produced by God in no other way, and in no other order than they have been produced' (*Ethics* IP16). So the infinite mode, 'the face [or 'make-up'] of the whole universe' is precisely that which is the object of 'God's idea', consonantly with the main thesis of Part II of *Ethics*, that any mode of thought is the idea of a corresponding mode of extension, with which it is identical. To spell the latter thesis out in another way favoured by Spinoza, the mind of any being is the idea of its body. God's idea of the universe, the complete idea of the universe *sub specie aeternitatis*, is thus rather closely equivalent, in his terms, to the Neoplatonic soul of the world.[28]

With respect to the infinite modes of extension, the teleological principle of descent from one level to another is clarified by another of Spinoza's responses to Tschirnhaus.[29] Tschirnhaus had asked[30] Spinoza for his explanation of how it can be deduced from the extension of matter that it is in motion, a key issue with respect to the orthodox notion of arbitrary and purposive creation. In addition to creating matter, it was thought, even on mechanist principles God would also have to put

---

[27] Cf. *Ethics* IP16: 'From the necessity of the divine nature there must follow infinitely many things in infinitely many modes (that is, everything that can fall under an infinite intellect).' (For an explanation of references to the works of Spinoza in this form, see Abbreviations p. ix.)

[28] The analogy is an old one, discussed, for example, by Leibniz in comments on Wachter on Spinoza: see G. W. Leibniz, *Philosophical Essays*, ed. and trans. R. Ariew and D. Garber (Indianapolis, IN: Hackett, 1989), p. 277.

[29] Letter 83, 15 July 1676.

[30] In letters 80 and 82, 2 May and 23 June 1676.

matter in motion in determinate ways, arbitrarily selected. It was in the context of this kind of point that Tschirnhaus argued that we cannot deduce the properties of anything from its essence alone, since any proof requires that we postulate other things. Thus we deduce the properties of a curve only by bringing it into relation with, for example, certain straight lines. Spinoza replied that indeed actual motion cannot be deduced from Descartes's definition of matter as extension, but that a better definition would be 'by an attribute that expresses an eternal and infinite essence'. Spinoza meant, I take it, that we need to take into account that what is extended is also perfect and infinite. Since it is less limiting and so better that what is extended is in (internal) motion than that it is entirely at rest, the perfect and infinite substance, conceived under the attribute of extension, will be in motion. And the mobile universe is informed, and so kept the same individual, by the laws of motion, and is configured eternally by just the infinity of motions that do affect it (that is, by all possible motions), because perfection requires that too.

His account of infinite modes effectively supplies Spinoza's solution, or dissolution, of the problem of the emanation or descent of finite, transitory particulars from what is infinite and eternal. Singular things are finite and determinate modes, that is to say, parts or constituents of the mediate infinite modes. The material universe consists of a unitary web of causally related finite modes of extension, that is to say, particular determinate motions, which are causally intelligible only as parts of the whole eternal and infinite configuration. Singular minds are finite and determinate parts or constituents of the idea of this web, that is to say, are parts of 'God's idea'.

Given all this, the very backbone of Spinoza's metaphysics, was Leon Roth right to propose that Spinoza came to Descartes's philosophy already a convinced monist? Spinoza's mature system evolved, on Roth's speculative analysis, as a way of abstracting Cartesian physics from Descartes's fundamentally pluralist system, and of finding a place for it within Neoplatonist monism in the Jewish tradition. In other words, his philosophy was not the result of the kind of critical development or improvement of Cartesian philosophy that many commentators have seen in it. One problem for Roth's view is that (as far as I know) there is no evidence of such pre-Cartesian Platonism on Spinoza's part. Spinoza's earliest extant writings on metaphysics are already deeply penetrated by Cartesian concepts. It therefore seems perfectly possible that he first read Descartes as an exciting modern philosopher working within the Platonist tradition with which he was himself already acquainted, and that he did so before plumping for a rigorous monism or, indeed, for any particular philosophical view whatsoever. It is just as likely that he was first inclined towards Platonic monism by particular features of Descartes's system, or by the desire to solve the problems that it sets, as that he had already been persuaded of monism by his teachers. It has been very plausibly suggested by a number of commentators, for example, that the most impressive of Spinoza's arguments for monism, the one most likely to reflect his own chief motive for it, lies in his assertion of the impossibility of the real or actual division of Cartesian extended substance: his appeal to the essential unity of Cartesian matter, every distinction within which is a function of its internal motion. It could well be that, in Spinoza's philosophical development, the Cartesian physics came first, the metaphysical monism later.

Naturalism and Spinoza's Epistemology

Nevertheless, it is certain that Spinoza brought to the critique, or improvement, or extravagant development of Cartesian metaphysics, however we regard it, ideas from Platonic monism that Descartes had largely ignored. Yet even that truth, or that part of the truth, may mislead. In what remains of this paper, I want to consider a third aspect of Spinoza's complex and ambiguous position. That is the point that his disagreements with Descartes were not just disagreements between one kind of Platonist and another, but can be taken to contribute to an argument aimed at the radical transformation, even subversion, of Platonism itself. One feature of this argument, of course, which received massive emphasis by his earliest critics, is his so-called 'materialism', his identification of God with matter, and of the soul with the body, which was taken to be just the kind of metaphysics to be expected from someone who attacked traditional religion and expounded radical political theory. The names of Hobbes and Spinoza became as closely linked, for some, as those of Peter and Paul. Yet Hobbes's general philosophy is about as far from Platonism as could be, and, from one point of view, to call both Hobbes and Spinoza 'materialists' might seem equivocation. But there is at least something to be said for assimilating the two philosophers, even with regard to their metaphysics. Spinoza's spectacular arguments for the dissolution of traditional dichotomies, the resolution of duality or multiplicity into unity, have as their outcome a philosophy that is profoundly naturalistic. God and nature, creator and creatures, matter and mind, thought and motion, thought and its object, divine ideas and human ideas, understanding and will, virtue and knowledge, even universals and particulars—all these dualisms are resolved into unities, often in ways that might seem calculated to disconcert not simply the traditionally religious or, for that matter, orthodox Cartesians, but any philosopher seriously within the Platonic tradition. Crudely, the question arises whether, in identifying God and nature, Spinoza was not more interested in naturalising Being than in recognising the world's divinity.[31]

Apart from the status given to matter or extension (and, after all, Henry More too envisaged an extended God, even if not a material one), grounds for supposing an intention actually to subvert traditional Platonism, rather than simply to develop a Cartesian Platonism in the direction of monism, can be found in Spinoza's epistemology. At first sight, and indeed beyond first sight, his theory of knowledge might well seem to have a firmly Cartesian–Platonist core. Sense gives only obscure and inadequate ideas of its objects, not knowledge. Imagination and memory give us experience of practical value, but without theoretical understanding. Reason has access to adequate ideas, enabling us to understand at least some things in the way they are understood by God. Moreover, as for Platonists generally, there is room for an even higher kind of knowledge, even more closely uniting us to God. Here is an expression of this last thought from a seventeenth-century writer:

[The true Metaphysical and Contemplative man,] running and shooting up

---

[31] Cf., e.g., Alan Donagan, 'Spinoza's Theology', in D. Garrett (ed.), *The Cambridge Companion to Spinoza* (Cambridge: Cambridge University Press, 1995), p. 355: 'Spinoza's theology, in short, naturalizes God.'

above his own *Logical* or *self-rational* life, pierceth into the *Highest life*: such a one, who by *Universal Love* and *Holy affection* abstracting himself from himself, endeavours the nearest Union with the Divine Essence that may be . . . To such an one the Platonists are wont to attribute . . . *a true divine wisdom.*[32]

What is this, we may ask, but Spinoza's 'intuitive knowledge', knowledge that proceeds from adequate ideas of divine attributes and gives rise to what he calls 'the intellectual love of God' (IIP40S2), knowledge that is equivalent in its way to Montaigne's true faith? If there is a difference, it might seem only to be that for Spinoza, as, I suppose, for Plato, such apprehension of the ultimate nature of being is not beyond or above human reason, but is simply the highest exercise of human reason.

Nevertheless Spinoza's epistemology has features that seem entirely out of place in a Platonist or a Cartesian. It is based on two ontological principles already mentioned, the proposition that the order and connection of ideas is the same as the order and connection of things, and the associated principle that the human mind is the idea of the human body. The latter entails that all thoughts, including universal or necessary thoughts as well as sense-perceptions and sensory imagination and memory, have something in the body as their immediate object. Certainly Spinoza allows for ideas of ideas, including ideas of the human mind. But, as we shall see, that is no qualification of the principle that the immediate object of any idea, of whatever kind, is the very mode of extension, that is to say, the motion in the body, with which that idea or thought is identical.

There was nothing new in the notion that *in sensation and imagination* the mind has something in the body or brain as its object. Indeed this can be seen as a view that Spinoza took over, *mutatis mutandis*,

---

[32] John Smith, *Select Discourses* (1660), p. 20. The passage is cited by E. S. de Beer, *The Correspondence of John Locke*, vol. 2, p. 489, in relation to an exchange between Locke and Damaris Cudworth (later Masham) in which Locke criticised Smith's conception. For comment on this exchange, see G. A. J. Rogers, 'Locke and Platonism' (forthcoming). For a more rationalistic, if still mystical, account of the supposed highest form of knowledge, compare Robert Greville, Lord Brooke, *The Nature of Truth: Its Union and Unity with the Soule, etc* (London: Samuel Cartright, 1641), p. 43.

from Descartes. In a number of passages[33] Descartes suggests his own version of a particular Aristotelian model. For Aristotelians, the active intellect turns to the corporeal imagination or common sense, a part of the brain, in order to form universal concepts from particular sensory representations. For Descartes, it does so in order to form intrinsically representational ideas involving or employing corporeal 'images', the immediate objects of the mind in sense-perception and imagination. Such images are constituted by motions in the brain, and are representational only in so far as they are referred by the mind to actual or supposed causes. Needless to say, there are problems with the model, which Descartes does not in any case keep to consistently. The present point is simply that the thought that mechanical occurrences in one's own body are the first or immediate objects of all sense and imagination is itself Cartesian.

I have mentioned Spinoza's famous difference from Descartes in his holding that occurrences in the body are not merely the immediate *objects* of representational thoughts or ideas, but are identical with those very ideas of which, conceived under the attribute of extension, they are the immediate objects. A connected, just as striking, difference from Descartes is that the model supplies Spinoza's account of our *adequate* ideas — that is, our perception of eternal truths, in the first instance eternal truths relating to bodies. Here the effective principle is that, even though our body is only a part of the universe, what we perceive to be true of it will be perceived as necessary and universal provided that the truth concerns what is common to both part and whole of any body and, in particular, what is common to our body and to other bodies. All bodies agree in certain respects, and in just those respects our idea of body is adequate. That is to say, our thought, the object of which is our own body, is no different in just those respects from God's thought, the object of which is the whole extended universe. That is the basis of Spinoza's explanation of the possibility of the *a priori* sciences of geometry and mechanics.

---

[33] Cf. *Treatise on Man* (AT XI 176–7; CSM I 106), *Meditations* VI (AT VII 73; CSM II). For discussion, see M. Ayers, 'Ideas and Objective Being', in *The Cambridge History of Seventeenth-Century Philosophy*, ed. D. Garber and M. Ayers (Cambridge: Cambridge University Press, 1998), pp. 1071–3.

Now one feature of this story is its dramatic effect on the Platonic triangle of divine ideas, human ideas and created essences in things, since it collapses the vertices of the triangle to a point. Briefly, since our minds are parts of the universal mind, our ideas are distinguished from divine ideas only as parts from a whole, but even that distinction cannot be drawn in the case of our adequate ideas. They simply *are* the divine ideas, which, in the case of our adequate ideas of body, are in turn identical with the universal aspects of body that are their object. That, presumably, is why Spinoza calls them 'adequate', a term Descartes had expressly limited to God's ideas, denying its application to the human.[34] Unsurprisingly, Edward Craig comments, 'Here we have the image of God doctrine in a very strong form indeed.'[35] Indeed, the intellectual love of God, as achieved by a human being, is, Spinoza asserts, 'the very love of God by which God loves himself'.[36]

Yet I have to say that another comparison than Craig's, and a very different one, comes to mind — a comparison that might raise some doubts about the Platonic credentials of Spinoza's explanation of *a priori* knowledge. For Hobbes too held that a process of analytical thought will enable us to identify those aspects or properties of perceived bodies that are common to all bodies and are, by the same token, the subject-matter of mechanical physics. If we conceive of bodies in terms of these most general, austerely mechanical properties, Hobbes claimed, the laws of physics will or can become evident to us.[37] In effect, Hobbes was explaining what he, by no means alone among empiricists of the time, regarded as the inherent intelligibility and necessity of mechanical processes and of the laws he supposed to govern them. He was asserting in effect that if in thought we strip perceived bodies down to what it is to be a body (that is, to what all bodies are and what bodies are essentially), then from this their powers and operations can be

---

[34] Fourth Set of Replies (AT VII 220; CSM II 155).
[35] *The Mind of God*, p. 48.
[36] *Ethics* VP36.
[37] *De Corpore* I vi 1–6. Hobbes apparently has in mind a kind of abstractive analysis of perceived bodies bringing us to the most simple and universal properties of bodies, a level at which causal principles become self-evident (*Causae . . . universalium . . . manifestae sunt per se*). The thought has antecedents in Stoic theory.

deduced.[38] Spinoza's explanation of the evident necessity of truths concerning properties common to all bodies, for all the references in its proof
to the divine mind, is at bottom much the same as that of Hobbes.

That might not seem particularly significant, since many[39] who
allowed necessity or *a priori* intelligibility to mechanical processes and
laws assumed that (at least, given motion) the operations of body flowed
from its essence. What is surely significant, however, is that Spinoza no
more than Hobbes treats the bodies perceived by sense (or images perceived by the imagination) to be mere prompts for the apprehension of
non-sensory ideas of a kind that are the peculiar objects of intellect,
whereas Plato's sharp distinction between the objects of intellect and the
objects of sense is of the essence of traditional Platonism. For both
Hobbes and Spinoza, the perceived body (for example, a diagram) or,
more immediately, its effect on our body (a physical image) serves as the
object of geometrical reasoning in so far as what is true of it is perceived
as true of bodies generally.

The two Propositions 38 and 39 of Part II of *Ethics*, in which Spinoza
presents his general explanation of the possibility of necessary or *a
priori* knowledge ('the cause of those notions . . . which are the foundations of our reasoning'), seem designed to stress the indispensable role of
sense and sensory images. Proposition 38 asserts that properties common
to all things, and equally in the part and whole of all things (i.e., in the
case of bodies, presumably, extension and motion) can only be perceived
adequately. Proposition 39[40] asserts, in effect, that when such common

[38] The general thought recurs, if appropriately weakened, even in the essentially more
sceptical philosophy of Locke. See, e.g., *Essay* II viii 9, where primary qualities are
described as 'such as Sense constantly finds in every particle of Matter, which has bulk
enough to be perceived, and the Mind finds inseparable from every particle of Matter,
though less than to make it self singly be perceived by our Senses'. Accordingly, 'the only
way which we can conceive Bodies operate in' is by impulse (*Essay* II viii 11).

[39] Many, but not all, in that Descartes and occasionalists in general assigned the laws to
God. As Cottingham points out in this volume (Chapter 2), that seems to imply that
mechanical processes are not inherently necessary or intelligible, and so to deny the
intuition.

[40] 'If something is common to, and peculiar to, the human body and certain external
bodies by which the human body is usually affected, and is equally in the part and in the
whole of each of them, its idea will also be adequate in the mind.' The Demonstration
makes clear that what is supposed is that the human body is affected by the external body

properties of bodies are perceived through the mechanism of sense-perception (that is to say, when external bodies affect the human body through those same properties), they are perceived adequately. So there are not, then (as it seems that there must be for Descartes[41]), two ways of perceiving (or having an idea of) extension, one sensory and the other intellectual, with a way of rising from the confusion and obscurity of the former to the clarity and distinctness of the latter. In effect, for Spinoza, every human mind always perceives extension and motion, and whatever follows from them, adequately, clearly and distinctly, and in no other way.[42] It does so both in so far as it perceives bodily images and external bodies, and in so far as it reflexively perceives its own ideas of these things.

It might seem tempting to regard Spinoza's account as in effect an explanation of how ideas of pure intellect, such as Cartesian innate ideas, are to be identified and made explicit. It is true that in various contexts he emphasises a difference between imagination and intellectual or abstract thought, between images and ideas: an image is a corporeal motion considered barely as such, whereas an idea is a mental affirmation. Yet the idea of a triangle necessarily involves, indeed *is*, a corporeal motion (which considered barely as such is an image of a triangle), and has that motion as its immediate object. In general, idea is to image as mind is to body — the same finite mode considered under

---

through the common property in question, i.e. through the physical mechanism of sense-perception.

[41] Descartes's answer to the question whether there are two ways of apprehending extension or just one is obscure — the answer 'Two, intellectual and sensory' is perhaps sometimes implicit, but in general the point seems to be left indeterminate. Malebranche tightens things up (or shifts the point of obscurity), answering 'One', firmly asserting that even in sense-perception extension is perceived by the intellect, with other qualities 'painted on' by sense. My suggestion is that Spinoza also answered 'One' — the common properties of bodies are perceived by sense, and are conceived of by means of sensory images.

[42] That is not, of course, to say that its ideas of *bodies*, including its own body, are adequate (cf. *Ethics* IIP24, for example). But every idea of every singular thing involves the idea of an attribute of which it is a mode (*Ethics* IIP45), and it is that idea that is adequate. Or as Spinoza has it, 'The knowledge of God's eternal and infinite essence which each idea involves is adequate and perfect' (IIP46).

different attributes (cf. *Ethics* IIP48S; IIP49CS). Accordingly, we can regard Spinoza's account of universal knowledge as a way of *avoiding* the Cartesian thesis that in physical science the mind rises entirely above sense-experience so as to grasp the mechanical properties of bodies in some purely intellectual way by 'turning to' its peculiar, non-sensory internal objects. If we choose to think of Spinoza's ideas of extension and motion as in some sense 'innate', that can only be in the sense that they are always with us, in all our contentful experience and thought. But that is just what the empiricist Hobbes also believed.

That our fully contentful thought (or thought considered concretely) is somehow tied to sense-experience and sensory images is also implied by Spinoza's account of the mind's knowledge of itself. The idea of the mind is the idea of the idea of the body, but this, Spinoza states explicitly, is not a distinct idea: it is simply what he calls 'the form of the idea [of the body] in so far as this is considered as a mode of thinking without relation to the object' (*Ethics* IIP21S). But of course every mode of thinking does *have* an object. As he goes on to say, 'The mind does not know itself, except in so far as it perceives the ideas of the affections of its body' (IIP23). In effect, in direct opposition to Descartes, he allows no way in which the mind can achieve knowledge of itself, or even form a concrete conception of itself, that is entirely separated from the corporeal as object.

Related points are, first, that if the infinite order of ideas constituting God's idea is not only identical with, but *of* the infinite order of things, the order of the mental realm, when adequately conceived, is reduced to being the order possessed by a true and full representation of the order of the physical realm. The intelligible order of ideas, it seems, simply charts the intelligible order of things.[43] Whether intentionally or not, that assigns a significant primacy to extension and physics over thought and mental causation. Second, upon close inspection Spinoza's 'intellectual love of God' might well look more like a clear-eyed, sober and sobering understanding that we exist as tiny, shifting parts of an utterly natural world

---

[43] Cf. Edwin Curley, *Behind the Geometrical Method* (Princeton, NJ: Princeton University Press, 1988), pp. 74–8.

than like the Platonists' ecstatic union with the Divine or vision of supernatural perfection.[44]

Conclusion

How, then, should we pick our way between, roughly speaking, Spinoza
the critical Cartesian, Spinoza the anti-Cartesian Platonist or
Neoplatonist, and Spinoza the radical proponent of naturalistic
materialism, or near-materialism? The first right step, very probably, is to
agree that he was, in one way and another, at least to some extent, all of
these things. That does some justice to the complexity and subtlety of his
thought, but does not, perhaps, get us very far towards identifying the
driving force in his philosophising — towards understanding what made
Spinoza tick. I follow others in supposing that that task requires us to turn
to the less metaphysical parts of *Ethics*, and to Spinoza's other writings.
There are already, of course, indications in those *scholia* in Parts I and II
of *Ethics* that excoriate certain *bêtes noires*: the idea or 'superstition' of
a personal God who acts arbitrarily, choosing between possibilities, who
created the world, and who cares for human beings, rewarding and
punishing them for their actions; and the idea that human beings, in
possessing free will, are not entirely parts of nature. These ideas, central
to traditional religion and morality, are, of course, flatly contrary to
Spinoza's metaphysics, but his opposition to them evidently stems from
more practical concerns, and from his analysis of the causes of human
error, wrongdoing and social discord. We may suppose that, contrary to
Marx's dictum, Spinoza wished not merely to understand the world, but
through the propagation of that understanding to change the way people
live and, above all, the way they live together — or fail to live together.
Like Plato, he wanted to show how the practice of virtue, the rational life,

[44] Catherine Wilson explores a related 'tension' in Spinoza's thought between a value-free
naturalism and a quasi-Platonic 'aspirational' ethics in 'The Strange Hybridity of
Spinoza's Ethics', in C. Mercer and E. O'Neill (eds.), *Early Modern Philosophy: Mind,
Matter and Metaphysics* (Oxford: Oxford University Press, 2006), pp. 86–102 (the title
is taken from a comment by Margaret Wilson). The combination might appear less
'strange' and 'puzzling' if placed in the context of the wider metaphysical programme.

is its own reward; and, like Plato, he wanted to draw from his analysis an account of the virtuous state, of 'how citizens are to be governed and led'. Yet within the self-consciously Platonic shell of his philosophy lies a message that subverts virtually everything that traditional Platonism stood for.

5

Comments on Ayers
'Spinoza, Platonism and Naturalism'

SARAH HUTTON

IN MY RESPONSE I shall focus on two points: first the sources of Spinoza's Platonism, and second his departure from Platonism — especially the claim that, the Platonist features of his thought notwithstanding, Spinoza's epistemology is deeply subversive of Platonism. I offer my comments more by way of a largely historical enrichment of the issues that Michael Ayers has raised than any serious disagreement about the discernible presence of Platonic elements in Spinoza. As will become apparent, however, I think a case can be made for Spinoza's having a stronger debt to Platonism, even in the area which Michael Ayers identifies as the least Platonic (even anti-Platonic) aspect of his philosophy.

In his concise and balanced discussion Ayers has demonstrated convincingly that, outwardly at least, Spinoza's philosophy exhibits many features that may be described as Platonist, and that this is particularly evident where Spinoza departs from Descartes. This being so, it is unlikely that Spinoza's Platonism was derived from Descartes. Ayers's list of the Platonist features of Spinoza's philosophical system includes the emanation of multiplicity from the singular perfection of the divine and the hierarchical ordering of substance and modes. He also suggests other echoes of Platonism — in particular Spinoza's rigorous pursuit of the unity of being, and a parallel between Spinoza's conception of *idea Dei* as the idea of the face of the whole universe with Plato's soul of the world. Furthermore, he acknowledges that Spinoza shared with Plato the desire to promote the practice of virtue through the rational life. This list of examples can be supplemented with others, for instance the points that

Proceedings of the British Academy, **149**, 79–89. © The British Academy 2007.

Spinoza's hierarchy of being rests on a correlation of perfection with reality, and expresses perfection in terms of action (*Ethics* VP40 and VP40D). Even his central claim that 'the order and connection of ideas is the same as the order and connection of things' (*Ethics* IIP7) may be construed in terms of the Neoplatonic hierarchy of being, while his claim that 'the human intellect is part of the infinite intellect of God' echoes the doctrine of the participation of the human mind in the divine mind. Predominant among these Platonic features of Spinoza's *Ethics* are doctrines that approximate more closely to the hierarchical metaphysics of later Platonism than to Plato himself. The least conclusion to be drawn is confirmation that Descartes's (rather perfunctory) Platonism was not a decisive factor in the attractiveness of his philosophy for Spinoza. Nevertheless, the presence of other elements in Spinoza's *Ethics*, especially, as Ayers argues, elements antithetical to Platonism, provokes the nagging question of whether the apparent Platonism of Spinoza is just a philosophical trick of the light, or whether it is something more deeply structural.

Sources

The question of whether Spinoza's philosophy is in any sense an outgrowth of the Platonic tradition is complicated by the notoriously difficult problem of reconstructing his philosophical background. Ayers leaves unanswered the question of the sources of Spinoza's Platonism, given that it was not wholly mediated through Descartes. Can we even be specific about sources? Spinoza studies have come a long way since the days of Roth and Wolfson. It is no longer assumed to be necessary to isolate his Jewish background from the Dutch intellectual context within which he lived, learned and practised philosophy.[1] Although we now

[1] Thanks to the work of Méchoulan, Kaplan and Popkin, far more is now known about seventeenth-century Judaism and its Dutch context. Henri Méchoulan, *Amsterdam au temps de Spinoza* (Paris: PUF, 1990); Yosef Kaplan, *From Christianity to Judaism. The Story of Isaac Orobio da Castro* (Oxford: Oxford University Press, 1989); R. H. Popkin, 'Christian Jews and Jewish Christians in the Seventeenth Century', in R. H. Popkin and G. M. Weiner (eds.), *Jewish Christians and Christian Jews* (Dordrecht: Kluwer, 1994).

know hugely more about that context, the question of his intellectual debts remains unresolved, both because he covered his traces so well, and because the history of his posthumous fortunes has obscured what we can learn from his *Nachlass*. The mere presence or absence of books in his library list is an unsafe guide to what he read. His extant letters afford important insights into his philosophy, but these letters are only a selection of what he wrote, and they are not much help on the subject of Platonism. A little may be inferred about the development of his philosophy from the chronological order of his extant writings, but none of these antedate his exposure to Cartesianism.

Alternatively, we may take a very broad view of the historical context and compare Spinoza with others of his contemporaries whose Platonism outstrips their Cartesianism — to see what we can learn from what might be called 'family resemblance' among these philosophers. Ayers rightly notes that the Platonism of the seventeenth century must be considered as multi-faceted, and that there was great diversity in the take-up of Platonist positions. Furthermore, as I am sure Ayers would agree, the philosophies of Plato and Plotinus were not mainstream philosophies in this period, even though the Platonic canon was vastly better known than in medieval times.[2] What now would be called the *Neo*platonic character of Spinoza's Platonism is very much in tune with Renaissance Platonism mediated by Ficino, who regarded Plotinus, the great systematiser of Platonic thought, as the true interpreter of Plato. In the wake of Ficino, early modern Platonism takes diverse forms ranging from *dialoghi d'amore*, such as the one by Leone Ebreo owned by Spinoza, to hefty philosophical syntheses, such as that set out in Cudworth's *True Intellectual System of the Universe*. Kabbalistic commentaries of the

Also, Jonathan I. Israel, *Dutch Jewry in the Age of Mercantilism 1550–1750* (Oxford: Oxford University Press, 1985), and, most recently, Stephen Nadler, *Spinoza. A Life* (Cambridge: Cambridge University Press, 1999). For the Dutch philosophical context, see Wiep van Bunge, *From Stevin to Spinoza*.

[2] P. O. Kristeller, *Eight Philosophers of the Italian Renaissance* (Stanford, CA: Stanford University Press, 1964); M. J. B. Allen, *The Platonism of Marsilio Ficino* (Berkeley, CA: University of California Press, 1989); James Hankins, *Plato in the Italian Renaissance*, 2 vols. (Leiden: Brill, 1990).

period are another example of systematised Platonism — albeit couched in mystical symbolic terms. There were also autodidacts, such as Jacob Boehme, whose direct knowledge of Platonism was probably minimal. At the other end of the scale, Platonism attracted the interest of humanist-educated professional academics, most of whom had theological concerns. In spite of the obscurities of the likes of Boehme, and the traditional theological objections to Platonism that go back to patristic times, Platonism had great attractions for those interested in the relationship of philosophy to theology, and of science or natural philosophy to religion. This is especially true of the Cambridge Platonists, who valued Platonism as a theistic philosophy compatible with the new natural philosophy of the seventeenth century. It is among this group that we find a penchant for Platonism accompanied by attraction to Cartesianism. John Smith (cited by Ayers) is a case in point.[3] Another good example is Henry More, who was initially, at least, attracted to Cartesianism as a means of securing the connection between theology and science. More was, however, critical of aspects of Cartesianism. In particular he did not think that Descartes had adequately explained the interaction of soul with body or of God with the world.[4] (His perception of the deficiencies of Cartesianism is therefore instructive in relation to Spinoza.)

When we turn to Spinoza's immediate context, we encounter the problem that, in the Netherlands at this time, Platonism was not a particularly popular philosophy. There is no equivalent to Cambridge Platonism among the Dutch. Stoicism was probably more widely known and studied in this period. Besides, Spinoza was himself dismissive of Platonists in general as well as of specific Platonist tenets. (For example, he rejects what he calls Plato's 'Universal Ideas' in the *Short Treatise*.) However, although there is not much evidence of a take-up of Platonic philosophy in the seventeenth-century Netherlands, interest in Kabbalism was strong in both the Jewish community and, increasingly,

[3] John Smith, *Select Discourses* (London, 1660).
[4] For More and Descartes, see Alan Gabbey, '*Philosophia cartesiana triumphata*. Henry More (1646–1671)', in T. M. Lennon, J. M. Nichols and J. W. Davis (eds.), *Problems in Cartesianism* (Kingston and Montreal: McGill-Queens University Press, 1977), pp. 171–249.

outside it. Spinoza acknowledged that he had read Kabbalistic writings, although he then dismissed Kabbalism as nonsense.[5] Nevertheless, one clue as to its relevance comes from the early reception of his philosophy, which was taken by many to have developed from Kabbalism.[6] This charge was, in some cases, made as an anti-Semitic smear. But, if we want an example of a 'dominant' non-philosophical discourse that had impact on serious philosophy (of the kind Edward Craig might propose), Kabbalism is just such a case. Kabbalism is, of course, a form of religious mysticism. But it was, none the less, an intellectual framework of sorts especially as explicated by Platonising commentators such as Abraham Cohen Herrera,[7] who was active in Amsterdam in the early seventeenth century, and whose work was known to Spinoza.

Spinoza was no Kabbalist, but in important details the Kabbalistical version of the Neoplatonic hierarchy fits the implicit hierarchy of the *Ethics* more closely than the Plotinian model — particularly in respect of pantheism and monism, supported as they are by an emanationist account of causality entailing continuous creation out of necessity of the divine nature. Also very suggestive of Kabbalism is Spinoza's reference in the *Short Treatise* to infinite understanding as 'a Son, product or immediate creature of God'. Ayers remarks that this has an oddly Trinitarian ring. But, it is, I think, more likely an allusion to Adam Kadmon than to the second person of the Trinity, particularly since *natura naturata* has not one, but two aspects, both of which Spinoza calls a 'son'. There seems to be a closer parallel between the dual functions of Spinoza's *natura naturata* and Adam Kadmon, the 'son of God' or 'celestial Adam' of

[5] *Tractatus theologico politicus*, ch. 9, in *Benedicti de Spinoza opera quotquot reperta sunt*, ed. J. van Vloten and J. P. N. Land, 4 vols. (The Hague: Nijhoff, 1964), vol. 2, p. 209.

[6] The first to pursue this thesis was Georg Wachter (1573–1677) in his book *De spinozismus im Judentum* (1699). See G. Scholem, 'Die Wachtersche Kontroverse über den Spinozismus und ihre Folgen', in K. Gründer and W. Schmitt-Biggemann (eds.), *Spinoza in der Frühzeit seiner religiosen Wirkung* (Heidelberg: Schneider, 1984), pp. 15–25. See also Jonathan I. Israel, *The Radical Enlightenment. Philosophy and the Making of Modernity* (Oxford: Oxford University Press, 2000). Wachter subsequently revised his view, in his *Elucidarius cabbalisticus* (1706).

[7] G. Scholem, *Major Trends in Jewish Mysticism* (New York: Schocken Books, 1974 (1946), and R. H. Popkin, *Spinoza* (Oxford: One World Publications, 2004), p. 83.

Kabbalist ontology.[8] Such Kabbalist echoes in Spinoza lend credence to Richard Popkin's claim that 'Spinoza, when looked at in terms of what he called the third kind of knowledge, can be read as a rational kabbalist shorn of imagery and numerology'.[9]

Even on Popkin's interpretation, however, Spinoza was no Kabbalist. But the presence among the discernibly Platonic aspects of Spinoza's philosophy of traits also found in Kabbalistic Neoplatonism has a number of consequences. First, it reinforces the evidence for Spinoza's debt to Platonism in general. Second, it points to a possible source for that Platonism in Spinoza's cultural background, one that probably antedates his acquaintance with Cartesian philosophy. Besides Kabbalism, this cultural heritage would include the Neoplatonism of Jewish thinkers such as Abraham Cohen Herrera and Leone Ebreo (Judah Leon Abravanel), as well as sources from Iberian traditions that formed part the *Marrano* heritage of Amsterdam Jewry.[10] Third, in view of the fact that these Kabbalistic/Neoplatonic elements derive from a form of religious Neoplatonism, the Platonism of Spinoza may be seen as an adaptation of Descartes's philosophy to fit an essentially Platonist account of God's relationship to the world, rather than as a development of the Platonic aspects of Cartesianism in a naturalistic direction. Viewed in that way, his enterprise was not so very different from that of Cudworth or More, or even Leibniz, who all sought a physics compatible with their theism. Spinoza's solution is, of course, radically different from theirs. But when we take account of the predominantly religious interpretation of Platonism in this period, and the likelihood that Spinoza employs (albeit in a non-mystical way) a highly religious version of it (namely Kabbalistic Neoplatonism), it is harder to sustain the case for Spinoza's naturalism.

---

[8] The *scholium* to *Ethics* IP29D echoes the account of *natura naturans* and *natura naturata* in *Short Treatise* 1.9, but omits any reference to production, or the 'son'. For philosophical interpretation of the Kabbalah, see Scholem, *Major Trends*, and Allison P. Coudert, *The Impact of the Kabbalah in the Seventeenth Century. The Life and Thought of Francis Mercury van Helmont (1614–1698)* (Leiden: Brill, 1999).

[9] Popkin, *Spinoza*, p. 83.

[10] E.g., Leone Ebreo's *Dialoghi d'Amore*, the one Neoplatonist work known to have been owned by Spinoza. It is essentially a work of Neoplatonist ethics, but includes a long discussion of epistemology.

Epistemology

Michael Ayers justly observes that there is much in Spinoza's philosophy that seems calculated to disconcert, not least the diversity of its constituents — be these Cartesian, Platonic or non-Platonic.[11] It is, therefore, reasonable to ask, as Ayers does, how the Platonic constituents sit with the rest, especially those that appear to be fundamentally at odds with Platonism. In particular, Spinoza's conception of thought and extension as the same thing, conceived under different attributes (*Ethics* IIP21), appears to imply that at all levels thought, ideas and mental process must, in a sense, be embodied. Spinoza's definition of mind as the idea of the body, and his claim that every idea has the body as its object, would seem to entail a materialist theory of knowledge. In that case Spinoza's epistemology would appear to be at odds with Plato's, and closer to Hobbes's, rather as his earliest detractors charged.[12] Henry Oldenburg probably had controversies surrounding Hobbes in mind when, in his second extant letter to Spinoza, he raises queries about Spinoza's understanding of the relationship of thought to extension, in the context of a contemporary debate as to whether thought is 'a corporeal motion or a spiritual activity quite distinct from what is corporeal' (*sitne motus corporeus, an actus quidam spiritualis, corporeo plane contradistinctus*). In his reply Spinoza denied that he held that thinking is a corporeal process ('actus corporeus'), but his denial was more than a little equivocal: 'So be it, although I make no such concession'.[13]

[11] This is echoed by Margaret Wilson in her remark that Spinoza's epistemology 'blends highly distinctive, original (even bizarre) formulations with both 'modern' — especially Cartesian—influences, and ideas and aspirations rooted in much older thought', 'Spinoza's Theory of Knowledge', in *The Cambridge Companion to Spinoza*, ed. Don Garrett (Cambridge: Cambridge University Press), p. 89.

[12] On the early reaction to Spinoza, see K. Gründer and W. Schmitt-Biggemann (eds.), *Spinoza in der Frühzeit*. Also Rosalie Colie, 'Spinoza in England, 1665–1730', *Proceedings of the American Philosophical Society*, 107 (1963), 183–219.

[13] Spinoza to Henry Oldenburg [October 1661], in *The Collected Works of Spinoza*, trans. Edwin Curley (Princeton, NJ: Princeton University Press, 1985), vol. 1, p. 171. For the Latin, *Benedicti de Spinoza, opera quotquot reperta sunt*, ed. J. van Vloten and J. P. N. Land (The Hague: Martinus Nijhoff, 1914), 3:8 and 10. Spinoza's denial is consistent with his repudiation in *Ethics* IIP49S of an impact theory of idea formation, according to which ideas are produced from traces in the brain 'formed in us from encounters with external bodies'.

The equivocation is perfectly explicable given that his position could not be accommodated by either of the two alternatives Oldenburg offered. But it is also consistent with the distinction Spinoza would wish to make between the physical or sensible body, conceived as inert matter, and the body understood as a finite, determinate component of the infinite order and connection of things.

Of course, that mind should have body as its object is not inconsistent with the doctrine that the mind of God contains the ideas of all things that exist in the physical world, and that human minds are finite versions of the divine mind. Likewise, Spinoza's definition of the order of nature in terms of extension echoes the primacy given to geometric order in the Platonic scheme of things. Furthermore, the fact that Spinoza allows a role for sense knowledge is not, of itself, un-Platonic. After all, since, for the Platonist, the world of things is a reflection of the divine mind, it affords even the most contemplative soul the basis for ascent to the divine. So, for example, Ralph Cudworth explains that it is through 'contemplation of corporeal things' that 'the intellectual mind . . . ascends to God'. And, as in Spinoza's account of the formation of the Common Notions, his Platonist contemporary, Ralph Cudworth, explains that the mind forms such notions by observing the 'passive prints and signatures' of God's order expressed in the physical world.[14] Spinoza's account of the cognitive ascent towards the 'intellectual love of God' entails the principle that the more perfect the understanding, the more removed it is from sense-experience — a principle far more suggestive of ancient Platonism than of his contemporary, Hobbes.

Leaving aside the many obvious differences between Hobbes and Spinoza (e.g., his account of the eternal mind which endures after the dissolution of the body), any assessment of Spinoza's epistemology must take seriously the qualifications and distinctions inherent in the epistemological framework that he outlines. In both the *Treatise on the Emendation of the Intellect* (*TIE*) and in *Ethics*, Spinoza goes to some lengths to distinguish between different types of knowledge, retain-

[14] Cudworth, *A Treatise Concerning Eternal and Immutable Morality*, ed. S. Hutton (Cambridge: Cambridge University Press, 1996), p. 96.

ing, in *Ethics*, the epistemological scheme outlined in the *Treatise*. There are also parallels between both works on the question of the human mind's apprehension of the universal properties of bodies. In both the ultimate goal of knowledge is knowledge of essences. According to the *Treatise* this is to be sought only from what Spinoza calls 'the fixed and eternal things' on which 'singular, changeable things' depend for their existence, and without which they cannot be conceived (*TIE* 101). To grasp the 'inmost essence' of things requires a higher order of intellection — the application of ideas 'from pure mind' ('ex pura mente' *TIE* 91). Correspondingly, in *Ethics* II Spinoza makes a distinction between the Common Notions which form 'the foundation of our reasoning' (*Ethics* IIP38) and the confused perceptions of the imagination which constitute the first kind of knowledge. Adequate knowledge of things yielded by the Common Notions is obtained not from the 'effects' of bodies in the 'common order of nature', but by grasping the what is 'common to all', namely causal principles or laws of nature that are unchanging, ubiquitous and everywhere the same — that is to say the principles of extension, motion and rest, but also, as Margaret Wilson points out, implicitly the principles of intellection or mentality.[15] In *Ethics*, no less than the *Treatise*, such knowledge entails an appeal (so to speak) to a higher order, that is to God 'in so far as he constitutes the human Mind' (e.g. IIP38D and P40D). Thus it is that 'it is the nature of Reason to regard things as necessary, not as contingent' (IIP44), and 'sub specie aeternitatis' (IIP44C2). Spinoza explains the nature of adequate ideas (IIP38–40), with specific reference to the Corollary of Proposition 11, 'that the human Mind is a part of the infinite intellect of God'. In other words, there is a sense in which Spinoza retains the Platonist epistemological doctrine of the participation of the mind in God. As Cudworth put it, true knowledge is possible by virtue of our minds being 'derivative participations of one infinite eternal mind'.[16] Furthermore, Spinoza's tripartite stratification of knowledge

---

[15] Wilson, 'Spinoza's Theory of Knowledge', p. 115.
[16] Cudworth, *Treatise*, p. 147.

in an ascending hierarchy is strongly suggestive of a Neoplatonic model.[17]

The Neoplatonist schema to which these elements point seems to me to offer a better fit between what Ayers calls the Platonic 'shell' and the apparently counter-Platonic content of Spinoza's theory of knowledge. Particularly relevant in this regard is the philosophy of Plotinus, whose systematised Platonism was hospitable to non-Platonic elements, especially Stoicism. Like Spinoza, Plotinus, in *Ennead* 1.1, outlines a tripartite stratification of knowledge, progressing from sense knowledge to reason and intellection. For Plotinus, the human being is 'joint entity', a compound of soul and body, where the soul itself has a higher and lower part. According to Plotinus, 'sense perception is a movement through the body which ends in the soul', and he explains how the soul perceives sense-impressions through the fact that living beings are compounds of body and soul. It is the whole person that thinks and feels, not any one part of this 'joint entity'. The soul, however, perceives not the objects of sense, but the intelligible entities or forms that are impressions produced from sensations, and which it grasps by reference to the archetypal forms of the intellect:

> Reasoning when it passes judgment on the impressions produced by sensation is at the same time contemplating forms and contemplating them by a kind of sympathy. I mean the reasoning which really belongs to the true soul: for true reasoning is an operation of acts of the intelligence, and there is often a resemblance and community between what is outside and within.[18]

The terms 'sympathy', 'resemblance', 'community' point to there being something in common between the body and soul ('what is outside and

---

[17] There is a striking Platonic parallel in his Platonist contemporary, John Smith, whose 'The True Way or Method of attaining Divine Knowledge' in his *Select Discourses* (London, 1660) outlines a similar progression from sense, through reason, to disembodied self-reflective reason, to divine love. For Smith and Spinoza on imagination, see S. Hutton, 'The Prophetic Imagination. A Comparative Study of Spinoza and the Cambridge Platonist, John Smith', in *Spinoza's Political and Theological Thought*, ed. C. De Deugd (Amsterdam: North Holland Publishing, 1984), pp. 73–81.

[18] *Ennead* 1.1.9, in *Plotinus*, trans. A. H. Armstrong, 7 vols., 2nd edn. (Cambridge, MA: Harvard University Press), vol. 1, p. 115.

within'), viewed differently according to whether it is apprehended by reason or sensation.[19] Reason grasps the forms individually ('unfolded or separated'), whereas intellect grasps them as a unity 'all together'. It is the forms that provide the basis of operations of the mind: 'From these forms . . . come reasonings, and opinions and acts of intuitive intelligence.'[20] Thus Plotinus's account of the formation of 'intelligible entities' or forms by reason in *Ennead* 1.1 bears comparison with Spinoza's account of the formation of the Common Notions, and their relationship to sense knowledge on the one hand, and *scientia intuitiva* on the other. At every stage of cognition, mind is embodied as part of the living being. This is true even of the intuitional insight afforded by the intellect, which entails contemplative ascent to the divine mind, whence intellect is derived.[21] Spinoza does not, of course, subscribe to the doctrine of the higher and lower soul. In any case he talks of mind (*mens*) rather than soul (*anima*). Spinoza's substance monism is, by any standards, a challenge to traditional views of Platonism, especially in its dualistic Christianised or Cartesian variants. But it bears resemblance to Plotinus's philosophical system (a parallel that was not lost on one of Spinoza's more discerning contemporaries, Pierre Bayle). My suggesting further Plotinian parallels with Spinoza does not answer the conundrum about his sources. Nor does it definitively settle the question of whether, overall, he can be considered as working within the Platonic tradition. But it does, I think, show that what Ayers refers to as 'the self-consciously Platonic shell' of Spinoza's philosophy owes more to Neoplatonic traditions than the parallel with Hobbes suggests.

---

[19] For further discussion, see Donald L. Ross, 'Plotinus the first Cartesian?' *Hermathena*, 169 (2000), 153–67. As it happens, the root of the term *koinonia* translated as 'community' is the same as for the original Greek term for the Common Notions, *koinai ennoiai*.
[20] *Ennead* 1.1.7, in *Plotinus*, trans. Armstrong, p. 109.
[21] See A. H. Armstrong, *An Introduction to Ancient Philosophy* (London: Methuen, 1972) (1947), pp. 192–3.

6

The Priority of the Perfect in the Philosophical Theology of the Continental Rationalists

ROBERT MERRIHEW ADAMS

IN THE THIRD OF HIS *MEDITATIONS*, Descartes says:

> And I ought not to think that I do not perceive the infinite by a true idea, but only by negation of the finite, as I perceive rest and shadows by negation of motion and light; for on the contrary I clearly understand that there is more reality in infinite than in finite substance, and that hence the perception of the infinite is in some way prior in me to that of the finite; that is, the perception of God is prior to the perception of myself. (AT VII 45)[1]

The conclusion of this passage astonishes readers today; it is so contrary to the modern tendency to seek to understand the more perfect, the more developed, in terms of the less perfect, the more rudimentary — to understand complex organisms, for instance, in terms of cells, cells in terms of molecules, molecules in terms of atoms, and the atoms in terms of subatomic particles.

It was not always so. That all things are to be understood in terms of their relation to the most perfect is a main theme of the Platonic tradition. And the modern determination to understand the more perfect in terms of the less perfect has roots in the rebellion against Aristotelian natural philosophy, and especially against its substantial forms that provided

[1] Cf. AT VII 113, 365. (For an explanation of references to the works of Descartes in this form, see Abbreviations, p. ix.) Although I have made some use of published English translations, I am in principle responsible for the translations from Latin and French in this essay.

Proceedings of the British Academy, **149**, 91–116. © The British Academy 2007.

principles of explanation — notably psychological and biological explanation — that could not be better understood by analysing complex beings
into simpler or more primitive beings. Descartes was a leader in that
revolution in natural philosophy, and famously reductionist in his
biology. All the more striking, then, that in his philosophical theology,
Descartes insists that the perception of the more perfect is prior to that of
the less perfect.

There is a philosophical question here which I think is not of solely
historical interest, though it will be viewed in this essay through a
historical lens. The question is this. Is the less perfect to be understood in
terms of the more perfect, or the more perfect in terms of the less perfect?
Like Descartes, we should not assume that the answer to this question
must be all or nothing either way. In our modern context it seems
obvious that a strategy of interpreting the more perfect or more
developed in terms of the less perfect or less developed — a 'bottom-up'
strategy, as we may call it — is appropriate and fruitful in many contexts.
But I think it is well worth exploring the hypothesis that there are also
important contexts in which a 'top-down' strategy of understanding and
representing the less perfect in terms of the more perfect or more complete will be the best.

Top-down strategies, in the indicated sense, are a persistent feature of
the philosophical theologies of major philosophers on the European
Continent in the early modern period — characteristic not only of Descartes,
but also of some of his most notable successors, including Spinoza,
Leibniz and Kant. Central to my own interest in the topic is a desire to
see how much sense can be made of the, at first sight rather strange,
notion of God as *ens perfectissimum* or *ens realissimum* that figures in
the work of Leibniz and Kant; and the machinery of the Leibnizian version of that idea will be a main subject of this paper. But I begin with the
rather different top-down strategies of Descartes and Spinoza.

Descartes

It is certainly not the case that top-down strategies were universally
favoured in philosophical theology in the early modern period. John

Locke, for instance, proposes a quite general bottom-up strategy for representing divine perfection. I believe this is deeply connected with Locke's empiricist opposition to Descartes's belief in innate ideas,[2] though this is not the place to explore issues about innatism. According to Locke, 'when we would frame an *Idea* the most suitable we can to the supreme Being, we enlarge . . . with our *Idea* of Infinity' all our ideas of qualities desirable in ourselves.[3]

A similar bottom-up strategy had already been proposed to Descartes as part of Pierre Gassendi's objections to the Third Meditation (AT VII 287) and something of the sort is also found in the 'Second Objections' to the *Meditations* (AT VII 123).[4] Such a strategy seems to work for some of the divine perfections most discussed in philosophical theology. Omniscience: I know some things, but God knows everything that's true. Omnipotence: I can accomplish some things, but God can accomplish absolutely anything that is intrinsically possible. Omnipresence and sempiternity: I am present at one place at a time, and have not been present at all at many times; but God is present at every place at every time. These are all cases in which the role of the 'idea of infinity', as Locke puts it, is assumed by universal quantification, which is used to generate a representation of a more perfect property from a representation of a quite ordinary property.

In other cases the role is assumed by the simpler machinery of negation. Imperishability and immutability: we know what it is for finite things to change and perish; God does not and cannot perish or even (on some views) change. Simplicity: God has no parts. Locke tells us to expect such negation in the construction of concepts of the perfect; for the idea of infinity is a negative construction on his view, 'the Negation of an end in any Quantity'.[5] Even the constructions using universal quan-

---

[2] I have developed this point at some length in Robert Merrihew Adams, 'Where Do Our Ideas Come From? — Descartes *vs.* Locke', in Stephen P. Stich (ed.), *Innate Ideas* (Berkeley and Los Angeles, CA: University of California Press, 1975), pp. 71–87, especially pp. 81–2.

[3] John Locke, *An Essay Concerning Human Understanding*, ed. Peter H. Nidditch (Oxford: Clarendon Press, 1975), II, xxiii, 33.

[4] The Objections are printed in AT together with Descartes's *Meditations*, as they were in his lifetime.

[5] Locke, *Essay*, II, xvii, 15.

tification have a negative aspect, for (as logicians know) the universal quantifier is implicitly negative. To say that God knows everything is to say that there is no fact that God does not know. Whatever facts God knows, it is essential to God's omniscience not only that God knows those facts, but also that there are no more facts to be known.

It was perceptive therefore of Descartes to associate the question whether the representation of the finite is prior to that of the infinite with the question whether the infinite is to be represented 'only by negation of the finite' (AT VII 45). To the extent that representations of divine perfections are constructible from more ordinary predicates by operations of negation and universal quantification, they are not prior to representations of less perfect things. Descartes claims that God's perfections are too positive to be constructible in that way. This claim is at the centre of an interesting argument against the possibility of a bottom-up construction of the idea of the infinite, which Descartes presents in a letter of August 1641 to 'Hyperaspistes'. It runs as follows (AT III 427):

1 'What makes the infinite different from the finite is something real and positive;
2 'on the other hand, however, the limitation which makes the finite different from the infinite is non-being or the negation of being.
3 'But that which is not cannot bring us to the knowledge of that which is . . .'
4 Therefore 'we do not understand the infinite by the negation of limitation.' (In other words, a negation or limitation of being does not provide, even by way of its own negation, the material for an understanding of a richer being.)

This seems to me a serious argument, whose premises have considerable plausibility. It cannot show, and perhaps is not meant to show, that a bottom-up approach cannot give us a negative concept of infinity which does indeed apply to God. But I think it does at least show how such a bottom-up strategy may be unable to give us more than a deficient understanding of the infinite, inasmuch as one who knows that the infinite contains more than the finite may still be far from knowing the more that it contains.

The obvious empiricist response to this argument is to deny that we can know the more that the infinite contains, and in that sense to deny that we can come to the knowledge of the infinite, in its superiority to the finite. Just such a denial is part of Gassendi's argument for a bottom-up approach to the concept of God:

> God [he says] is certainly infinite distances above every concept; and when our mind prepares itself to contemplate him, it is not only clouded in darkness but is reduced to nothing . . . [I]t is more than enough if . . . we can derive and construct an idea of some sort for our own use . . . which does not transcend a human concept and which contains no reality except what we perceive in other things or as a result of encountering other things. (AT VII 287–8)

It is easy to read Descartes as yielding ground to Gassendi on this point. He agrees — indeed emphasises — that our understanding of the divine perfection is extremely incomplete; and there are actually several texts in which he seems to admit a bottom-up approach by allowing that the human mind has the ability to represent divine perfections by 'amplifying' its ideas of the limited perfections of finite things.[6] He usually goes on to argue that our faculty of amplifying our ideas shows that our mind, which possesses it, must have been created by God (AT III 64, 427–8; VII 370–71) — a conclusion that, if granted, is well suited to the causal argument of the Third Meditation. It does nothing, however, to sustain the necessity, or even the possibility, of a top-down strategy in understanding the constitution of finite and infinite perfections.

Descartes was probably less interested in the top-down strategy than in the causal argument for theism. There is one passage, however, in his response to Gassendi, in which he proposes an inference in which our faculty of amplifying ideas of limited perfections is treated as evidence supporting a top-down approach, presupposing not only a causal dependence on God, but also an idea of God's perfection. Descartes asks, 'how could we have a faculty for amplifying all created perfections . . . were it not for the fact that there is in us an idea of something greater, namely God?' (AT VII 365).

---

[6] AT III 64, 427–8; VII 137–9, 365, 370–71. Jean-Luc Marion, *Sur la théologie blanche de Descartes*, 2nd edn. (Paris: Presses Universitaires de France, 1981), pp. 393–4, has been helpful in locating these texts.

Why would a faculty of amplifying ideas of limited perfections pre-
suppose an idea of infinite perfection? The most interesting answer to this
question offered by Descartes comes from a letter to Clerselier, dated 23
April 1649, only months before his death.

> Now I say that the notion I have of the infinite is in me before that of the
> finite, for just from the fact that I conceive being or that which is, without
> thinking whether it is finite or infinite, it follows that it is infinite being that
> I conceive; but in order to be able to conceive a finite being, I must cut
> back something from that general notion of being, which therefore must
> precede it.[7]

Here the general notion of being, the notion of being as such or of being
pure and simple, is identified with that of infinite being. The conception
of a finite being depends on that of infinite being because it contains the
general notion of being, which *is* that of infinite being. We may conceive
of being in a general way 'without thinking whether it is finite or
infinite'; implicitly, however, it is infinite being that we conceive in this
way, for the conception of a finite being is constructed from that of
infinite being by taking something away from it. This is plainly a top-
down construction of the notion of finite being.

I do not suppose that being is the only property whose perfection
Descartes would understand in a top-down way. I think Stephen Menn is
probably right in arguing that Descartes understands the perfections of
mentality in a similar way, though that does not seem unambiguously
implied in the texts. But what Descartes offers us in this way is not a
general theory of the derivability of the constitutive properties of finite
things from those of the infinite being. Such a general, top-down theory
of the constitution of the properties of things will be part of the philosophies of Spinoza and Leibniz, but it is blocked in Descartes's philosophy
by the thesis that some of the limited perfections of finite things are not
present in God formally, but only eminently.

It is clear that this restriction is motivated at least partly by
Descartes's commitment to the incorporeality of God. Corporeality, he
says, is not to be ascribed to God because it implies divisibility, which is

---

[7] AT V 356, cited by Stephen Menn, *Descartes and Augustine* (Cambridge: Cambridge
University Press, 1998), pp. 284–5. My translation largely agrees with Menn's.

an imperfection (AT VII 138). Extension, which for Descartes is the essence of body, and the ground of its divisibility, must be denied of God for the same reason. All this is reflected in his saying,

> We also recognise that among several unlimited particulars of which we have the ideas, such as unlimited or infinite knowledge; likewise infinite power, number, length, etc.; there are some, such as knowledge and power, that are contained formally in the idea that we have of God, and others, such as number and length, that are in it only eminently. (AT VII 137)

In this statement Descartes speaks of properties contained formally or eminently in the *idea* of God; but our best guide to understanding the distinction is probably his most explicit definition of it, in a closely linked text, as applied to containment in *objects* of ideas:

> The same things are said to be in the objects of our ideas *formally* when they are of the same sort in the objects as we perceive them to be; and *eminently* when they are not really of the same sort but are so great that they can fill the role of such things.[8]

Putting these texts together, we may plausibly ascribe to Descartes the following view. Unlimited being, knowledge and power are contained in the idea of God (and indeed in God) in a way that corresponds exactly to our perception of them. These unlimited divine attributes are also constituents, and indeed the positive content, of our ideas of limited being, knowledge and power, which add to them nothing but limits. No divine perfection, however, stands in that relationship to extension, or its modes, such as length. What there is in God that corresponds to their limited perfections is something (a being and a power) that is great enough and perfect enough to fill a certain role, which I think must be that of *causing* those limited perfections and our ideas of them; but it does not contain any of the specific positive content that distinguishes extension from other attributes. Extension cannot be constructed from an attribute of God as limited knowledge, power and being can be constructed from their unlimited counterparts.

[8] AT VII 161. The Latin of this passage requires a somewhat free translation; I have been guided in mine partly by the authorised French translation that appeared in Descartes's lifetime (AT IX 125).

Concluding this discussion of Descartes I'll mention three problems about his position. The first arises from the fact that he says that no attributes belong univocally to God and to us. The reason for this, as for many similar claims in the Middle Ages, is not simply God's transcendent greatness, but a doctrine of divine simplicity according to which no attributes are really distinct from each other in God, as they typically are in us. How this denial of univocity is supposed to be consistent (as Descartes must have supposed it to be) with the claim that some attributes of finite things are contained formally (though without their limits) in the idea of God is a question I shall not address here.

A central feature of Descartes's view, as I have sketched it, is the thesis that infinite being, and I suppose also infinite knowledge (omniscience) and infinite power (omnipotence) *are* being, knowledge and power as such, the objects of the general ideas of being, knowledge and power. A second problem for Descartes is whether that thesis is correct, or even plausible. I doubt that we can glean much satisfying argument about it from him, but I will return to pretty much the same question in connection with Leibniz.

In the third place, there is at least the appearance of a problem here for Descartes's dualism. It seems the positive content that constitutes the formal and objective reality (or thinghood) of body cannot be derived from the divine attributes as that which constitutes the formal and objective reality of mind can. There is thus a fundamental ontological disparity between them. It is noteworthy that Spinoza and Leibniz, who emphasise the derivability of the properties of the finite from those of the infinite, abandon one or another of Descartes's views that seem to clash at this point. Spinoza allows extension and thought to be in God in the same way, and Leibniz does not allow extension to constitute a substance or thing in itself at all.

Spinoza

I read Spinoza as a strong, but atypical, and highly original, exponent of a top-down treatment of the relation between the attributes of infinite and finite beings. Descartes was of course not the first to offer a top-down treatment of that relation. The archetypal top-down treatment in Western philosophy is Plato's, and it is echoed in much of philosophical theology from late antiquity through the Middle Ages. Of the relations suggested by Plato as obtaining between ordinary particulars and the Forms, the one most used in structuring philosophical theologies has been that of an imitation or imperfect copy to an archetype or exemplar; and something like that is envisaged in Descartes's top-down approach. In Spinoza's conception of how the properties of God are prior to the properties of finite things, the exemplar/imitation relation is replaced by the substance/mode relation (borrowed, after a fashion, from another aspect of Descartes's philosophy).

At the centre of Spinoza's conception of the relation of finite things to God is what we may call the relation of *modification*, the relation of modes, not only to substance, but also to attributes. For Spinoza a mode of an attribute is no longer merely a *way* of having that attribute, for the classification of properties of finite things as modes in that sense does not obviously have the monistic implications of Spinoza's conception of the mode/attribute relation. It is tempting to say that for Spinoza finite modes of extension and of thought are modifications that constitute *parts* of the infinite systems that are concretely and respectively the divine extension and thought; and certainly one important feature of the relationship for Spinoza is that each finite mode is included in the divine substance, under its attribute, along with infinitely more that is not included in that finite mode. The finite modes are related to the substance as incomplete to complete. They are partial expressions of the divine attributes.

However, Spinoza famously denies that God has parts. The denial is thought out in terms of a rather specialised conception of parthood, defined by the criterion that 'A thing composed of different parts must be such that each singular part can be conceived and understood without the others' — and could indeed, at least intelligibly, exist without the others.[9] Indeed, Spinoza's argument that extended substance does not satisfy this criterion for having parts provides one way of understanding, at least

---

[9] *Opera* I 24–5 (*Short Treatise*, I, ii). (For an explanation of references to the works of Spinoza in this form, see Abbreviations, p. ix.) I quote from Curley's translation of the *Short Treatise*.

with respect to the attribute of extension, how the infinite is prior to the finite. Accepting Descartes's argument that extension's role as essence of a substance excludes the possibility of a vacuum or empty space, Spinoza argues that therefore it is impossible for one part of an extended substance to 'be annihilated, the rest remaining connected with one another as before', and hence that the supposed parts of extended substance satisfy neither his criterion of parthood nor the traditional criterion of real distinctness (*Opera* II 59: *Ethics* IP15S). In this way the whole is prior to the supposed parts, or more fundamental than they are. They cannot be anything at all except as they have a place in the system that constitutes the complete extended substance.

Similarly, in the attribute of thought, Spinoza regards the finite modes, such as our minds, as essentially fragments of the infinite intellect of God, and none of them can be completely understood without understanding the whole system. Spinoza even says that 'the human mind is a part of the infinite intellect of God' (*Opera* II 94: *Ethics* IIP11C). That infinite intellect is not, for Spinoza, the thinking substance, but an infinite mode thereof. His view seems to be that the finite mode is a part, not of the infinite substance as such, but rather of the whole (infinite) *way* in which the substance is modified under one of its attributes.

Underlining the part/whole relation between the human and divine intellects, Martial Gueroult rightly makes the point that the difference between them is quantitative rather than qualitative.

> My intellect is not an *effect*, but a *part*, of the divine intellect . . . Thanks to that commensurability [between the part and the whole], God's knowledge, that is, the truth, differs from man's knowledge, not in *nature*, but only in *quantity*.[10]

Thus thought and extension are predicated univocally of finite things and God. What they *are* is the same in finite things as it is in God, or at least in the infinite and eternal modes of God.[11] The difference is just that the

---

[10] Martial Gueroult, *Spinoza*, vol. I: *Dieu (Éthique, I)* (Paris: Aubier-Montaigne, 1968), p. 404.

[11] Spinoza says that 'God's intellect, *in so far as it is conceived to constitute the divine essence*, differs from our intellect both as to its essence and as to its existence, and

thought or the extension that is in a finite thing does not contain the complete system of thinking or extended being that is in God.

Spinoza does not apply this schema of relations between finite and infinite to all the attributes traditionally attributed to God, but only to thought and extension, among attributes of which we have any conception. In his early *Short Treatise*, Spinoza says that '*existing of itself, being the cause of all things, the greatest good, eternal*, and *immutable*, etc.' do indeed belong to God as '*propria*' of God, but are not 'attributes' of God. As *propria* they belong to God alone, and Spinoza is not committed to finite things' having properties of the same nature with them.

He is arguing here against scholastic philosophers who held 'that God cannot be defined because the definition must represent the thing absolutely and affirmatively, and in their view one cannot know God affirmatively, but only negatively'; and doubtless Spinoza regards extension and thought as attributes that have positive content. So it is tempting to suppose that Spinoza's reason for regarding the mentioned properties as non-attributes is that they are negative. But I have not found that he says exactly that, and in fact not all of them are clearly negative. Existing of itself and causing all things do not seem purely negative, and similar questions could be raised about unity and infinity, mentioned by Spinoza in a note. What seems common to all the properties classified here as *propria* but not attributes of God is something harder to sum up in a word. They are relative, structural, formal, or in some cases negative properties. Spinoza's central point about them is probably best expressed by him when he says that the mentioned non-attributes are 'only *Propria*, which indeed belong to a thing, but never explain what it is . . . [T]hrough those *propria* we can know neither what the being to which these *propria* belong is, nor what attributes it has.' In Aristotelian terms, they do not answer the question, 'What is it?' which must be answered by whatever

---

cannot agree with it in anything except in name' (*Opera*, II 63: *Ethics* IP17S, emphasis mine). I am indebted to Michael Della Rocca for pointing out to me that Spinoza does *not* make a similar denial regarding the divine intellect conceived as an infinite and eternal *mode* of God; this is a correction of Robert Merrihew Adams, *Leibniz: Determinist, Theist, Idealist* (New York: Oxford University Press, 1994), pp. 21 and 125–6.

attributes constitute a thing as a substance — a question to which Spinoza believes that the Cartesian attributes of thought and extension provide the only answers known to us.[12]

Leibniz

Unlike Spinoza (and Descartes), the mature Leibniz does not think that extension can explain what a thing that has it is. By the 1690s we find him arguing that extension cannot be, as Descartes held, the essence of a substance because it is only a structure of relations, 'a repetition or continuous multiplicity of that which is spread out . . . and consequently it does not suffice to explain the very nature of the substance that is spread out or repeated, whose notion is prior to that of its repetition'.[13] Although Leibniz does not make the theological link explicit, this argument clears a way for holding that extension is not a divine attribute[14] while also maintaining a general top-down theory of the constitution of the properties of things.

In such a theory Leibniz too is concerned with properties viewed as able to explain what the thing *is* that has them. In terminology that is used by all the philosophers we are discussing, we are concerned with properties that can constitute the *reality* of a thing. To say that a thing has reality, in the sense that concerns us here, is not to say only that there is such a thing, and does not always imply that it actually exists. 'Reality',

[12] The source of all the quotations and citations in this paragraph and the one preceding it is Spinoza, *Opera* I 44–5 (*Short Treatise* I vii); I quote from Curley's translation of the *Short Treatise*. The passage receives an illuminating discussion in Alan Donagan, 'Spinoza's Theology', in Don Garrett (ed.), *The Cambridge Companion to Spinoza* (Cambridge: Cambridge University Press, 1996), pp. 343–82 (in particular, pp. 346–8).

[13] G IV, 467/W 104 (published January 1693). A similar argument is found in G IV, 364f./L 390 (1692 or earlier), in G II, 169f., 183/L 516, 519 (1699), in G IV, 589 (1702), in G VI, 584, and in several other texts. (For an explanation of references to the works of Leibniz in this form, see Abbreviations, p. ix.)

[14] By his last years Leibniz seems not to ascribe to God any attribute that is a version of extension or spatiality. Even immensity, the divine attribute he associates most closely with space, appears to be no more than an aspect of the divine omnipotence. But this is by no means so clear in Leibniz's early writings. For a sketch of the development of his views on the subject, see Adams, *Leibniz*, pp. 123–4.

or in Latin *realitas*, is an abstract noun formed from the noun *res* or 'thing' in such a way that it can mean *thingishness* or *thinghood*. We are concerned here with what is required to constitute something as a *thing*.

This opens the door to speaking, as all of our authors do, of things having more and less reality. The question, 'Is there such a thing?' seems to require the answer 'Yes' or 'No' — not 'More', and not 'Less'. But things may be more and less richly endowed with thingishness, if what constitute them as things are properties or attributes that vary in degree or may be possessed more or less completely or perfectly, as all of our authors suppose.

This supposition is closely connected with doctrines of the priority of the infinite. In the Third Meditation, for example, it is from his understanding 'that there is more reality in infinite than in finite substance' that Descartes infers that 'the perception of the infinite is in some way prior in me to that of the finite'. And, as we see in the same text, having 'more reality' is something that goes beyond any mere 'negation of the finite' (AT VII 45). It is something positive and, in Spinoza's terms, it explains *what* the thing that has it *is*.

It is in terms of this conception of 'reality' that we must understand Leibniz when he says that 'all the reality of creatures is in God'.[15] He is saying that the positive content of the properties that constitute the thingishness of finite things is somehow in God. I don't think this can mean a connection as loose as the 'eminent' containment allowed by Descartes. For Leibniz proposes, as Descartes does not, a *general* top-down theory of the *constitution* (and not just the causation) of the constitutive properties, or *realities*, of finite things as deriving their positive content from those of the infinite being, a theory that I think entails more commonality of nature between finite and infinite than Descartes requires.

At the same time Leibniz must affirm less sameness of nature between the attributes of finite and infinite beings than Spinoza affirms, if he is to distance himself from Spinoza's pantheism, in which a divine attribute actualises itself in a system of which finite things are fragments. To be sure, there are relatively early texts, from his Paris period, in which

---

[15] A VI, iv, 990. (For an explanation, see Abbreviations, p. ix.)

Leibniz seems at least tempted by a view similar to Spinoza's.[16] From 1678 on, however, he clearly rejects pantheism, insisting in the end on a difference in nature between God and finite things, or creatures: 'the reality of creatures', he says, 'is not that same absolute reality that is in God, but a limited reality, for that is of the essence of a creature'.[17] Lacking perfections essential to God, and possessing limited or imperfect properties that do not characterise God, creatures must therefore be distinct from God by what is often called 'Leibniz's Law' of the numerical difference of things that are qualitatively different.

How can Leibniz maintain both the commonality of nature and the difference of nature that he requires? Leibniz's top-down approach to the relation between the attributes of the finite and the infinite is articulated in his conception of God as the *ens perfectissimum*, the most perfect being, 'a subject of all perfections'.[18] As this formulation suggests, Leibniz, unlike Descartes, speaks without embarrassment of God as having a plurality of distinct properties. He maintains that God is simple, but in the same sense in which all the monads or fundamental substances of his system are simple — that is, in the sense of having no parts that are or could be substances.[19] Properties, distinct from each other as they may be,

---

[16] These are discussed at length in Adams, *Leibniz*, pp. 123–30.

[17] A VI, iv, 990, correcting the translation given in Adams, *Leibniz*, p. 133. The development of Leibniz's thought on these points is traced much more fully in *ibid.*, pp. 123–34.

[18] A VI, iii, 579/L 167.

[19] For the plurality of properties in God, see A VI, iii, 519–21, Gr 557; for a possible hesitation about it, see G I, 140 = A VI, iv, 1766 (probably of 1678). For the assimilation of God's simplicity to that of finite monads, see Gr 557, G VI, 576. (For an explanation, see Abbreviations, p. ix.) For a comprehensive discussion of divine simplicity in Leibniz, see Gaston Grua, *Jurisprudence universelle et théodicée selon Leibniz* (Paris: Presses Universitaires de France, 1953), pp. 274–88. Grua seems a bit scandalised by Leibniz's apparent acceptance of a real plurality of attributes in God, and sees in Leibniz more evidence than I do of hesitation about it. Leibniz may have been an innovator on this point, as Grua (*ibid.*, p. 274) suggests that he was on the related identification of the elements of creaturely properties, 'except for their limitations, with the attributes or perfections of God'. The modified version of divine simplicity is seen in full explicitness in the mid-eighteenth century in the broadly Leibnizian *Metaphysica* of Alexander Gottlieb Baumgarten (7th edn., Halle: Hemmerde, 1779; reprint Hildesheim: Georg Olms, 1963), which Kant used year after year as a textbook for his lectures on metaphysics. Baumgarten holds that 'there is . . . in the most perfect being a certain absolutely necessary plurality' (§803). And 'given the supreme simplicity of God, his being com-

do not count for Leibniz as parts that could disturb the simplicity of a substance.

But what is a perfection? 'A *perfection*', Leibniz says, 'is what I call every simple quality that is positive and absolute', where an absolute quality is one 'that expresses without any limits whatever it expresses' (A VI, iii, 578/L 167). Properties that are to be perfections, according to this definition, must satisfy four conditions.[20] (1) They must be qualities rather than, say, relations. (2) They must be simple. (3) They must be positive — metaphysically and not just verbally. And (4) they must be absolute; that is, they must express or possess their content, their reality, 'without any limits'.

Absoluteness is an intensification of positiveness, for limitation is conceived here as partial negation; and it is the most constant feature of Leibniz's conception of perfections that they are so purely positive as to involve no negation at all[21] — by which I assume is meant, no limitation of their possession or expression of their positive qualitative content.

Simplicity, as a property of perfections, is not essential to Leibniz's version of the ontological argument for the existence of God,[22] and is therefore omitted from some of his definitions of a perfection.[23] Simple properties play a crucial role, however, in his top-down understanding of the constitution of the properties of things. Leibniz is as insistent as Descartes that the perfect, the unlimited, the 'absolute', is conceptually prior to the imperfect. He tries to combine this with the characteristic-ally though not exclusively modern penchant for trying to understand the

---

posed in any way of parts outside of parts is indeed excluded, but a most real diversity of a plurality in God is not excluded, since even in finite things it is false that all things really diverse are set outside each other' (§838).

[20] For a fuller discussion of the interpretation of this definition, see Adams, *Leibniz*, pp. 113–19.

[21] See his *Monadology*, §§41, 45.

[22] See Adams, *Leibniz*, pp. 145–6.

[23] As when he says in his *Theodicy* (1710) that 'every reality that is purely positive or absolute is a perfection' [G VI, 383/p. 54 in the English translation by E. M. Huggard (London: Routledge & Kegan Paul, 1951)]. A similar definition is in A VI, iv, 556 (probably of 1683–5); cf. Donald Rutherford, *Leibniz and the Rational Order of Nature* (Cambridge: Cambridge University Press, 1995), p. 24.

complex in terms of the simple — and, indeed, with a sort of atomism about concepts, though not about physical objects. This is signalled when he says that 'the absolute concept is always prior to, and simpler than, the limited'.[24]

It is important both to Leibniz's metaphysics and to his philosophy of logic that he thinks of all properties or concepts as either simple or constructed from simple predicates by logical operations such as conjunction and negation. Even though positive predicates don't have to be simple, all the simple predicates are positive. For since negation is a logical operation rather than a predicate with non-logical content, the absolutely simple predicates, which are not constructed by any logical operation, will not involve any negation, and will thus be absolutely positive. All simple qualities will therefore be perfections by Leibniz's definition; and Leibniz seems in fact to have believed that all the simple predicates, of which all other predicates are ultimately composed, are among the attributes of God, even if he sometimes counts conjunctions of such simple predicates, without any negation or limitation, as divine perfections too. On this view, the less than perfect properties of finite things must all be composed, by logical operations including various degrees of limitation or partial negation, from the simple perfections of God. That, I take it, is the structure of Leibniz's most articulated top-down conception of the constitution of the properties of things.

I wish to explore here two issues about it. First, can the positive qualities of finite things in fact be constructed, in a way that fits Leibniz's strategy, as limited degrees of positive qualities that in God are absolute or unlimited? Second, how plausible is it to identify the simple qualities (if there are any) with the divine perfections?

Constructing the Positive Qualities of the Finite

In evaluating the success of Leibniz's top-down construction of positive qualities of creatures as limited degrees of absolute attributes of God, let's begin with an example both Descartes and Leibniz would like: pure

[24] Leibniz, A VI, iv, 2314 (the Academy editors argue for a date of about 1685); cf. A VI, iii, 502 (1676) and A VI, vi, 157f. (in Leibniz's *New Essays Concerning Human Understanding*, c. 1704).

primordial power, considered both as omnipotence and as a simple, purely positive quality. It is questionable whether any power can be both omnipotence and a simple, purely positive quality; but let's postpone worrying about that objection.

In logical construction Leibniz often gives the impression of wanting to use only truth-functional logical operators — particularly negation and conjunction. Strict adherence to this austere aspiration would leave him with a stark choice between two alternatives regarding the relation between the powers of finite things and the simple, purely positive, and therefore perfect power of God from which (on Leibniz's view) they are constructed: either the finite things have that same perfect power that God has, or they have the negation of it. Neither alternative is attractive. If the finite things have the negation of the primordial divine power, it is hard to see what property they can have that is constructed from that power by negation and conjunction except absolute powerlessness. But they are not supposed to be absolutely powerless. On the other hand, if they have that very property that is pure primordial power, unmodified by negation, then it seems they have one of the perfect attributes of God, even if it is conjoined in them with negation of other perfections. But finite things are not supposed to have any of those perfect attributes.

There is some indication that Leibniz would not in fact restrict himself rigorously to truth-functional constructions.[25] And surely neither of the two alternatives offered by such a construction for the limitation of divine perfections in creatures accords with Leibniz's intentions. Limitation, I have suggested, is partial negation; and *partial* negation is exactly what is wanted here. On a Leibnizian account the perfection of power should be partly denied and partly affirmed of finite things. But how can an absolutely *simple* property be partly denied of anything? What part of it is to be denied, and what part affirmed, given that it has no parts at all? If a simple property is to be affirmed or denied of something, it would seem that it must be affirmed or denied as a whole. But can a property be partly affirmed or denied as a whole?

Perhaps it can. Perhaps indeed we routinely do that with *compara-*

---

[25] See C 358–9, where Leibniz seems to accept non-truth-functional constructions employing 'particles' such as 'in'.

tives. If I say that pineapples taste sweeter than bananas, though both are sweet, I do not imply that there is some *part* of (phenomenal) sweetness that is present in the experienced flavour of pineapples but missing from that of bananas. I can and do say that bananas are *less* sweet than pineapples without presupposing any analysis of sweetness into parts. 'Less sweet' functions here as a partial negation, one which implies 'not as sweet as the comparison case' but does not imply 'not sweet at all'. This comparative sort of partial negation is not a truth-functional connective, but in another way it seems to be exactly what we are looking for. After all, the relation of finite things to God with respect to power is precisely that they are *less powerful* than God.

How would a comparative construction work for Leibniz? Suppose God has the pure and simple perfection of power (= **P**). Suppose further that there is a creature that is one-billionth as powerful as God, and thus has the one-billionth degree of **P**. There is a fairly obvious theological objection to this way of beginning a construction. God's power and knowledge are commonly thought to be *immeasurably* greater and more perfect than any creature's. Is it theologically acceptable to suppose that any creature's power or knowledge is one-billionth as great and perfect as God's? — or one over ten to the nth for any value of n? This might seem to be merely a problem about a particular device of presentation; but I rather doubt that any comparative construction that would be sufficient to determine a property of a finite thing would be theologically acceptable if the one I have begun to sketch is not. Here I won't dwell on this theological objection, however, because my present project has to do rather broadly with philosophical availability and unavailability of constructions.

If we suppose, then, that some finite being has power one-billionth as great as pure and simple **P**, a Leibnizian may construe this creature's property of power as a complex property whose constituents are: **P**, and the limiting or partly negative property-forming operator *the one-billionth degree of*. The possessor of this property does *not possess* **P**. For one thing, the degree-possessing is a complex property, and **P** is a simple property. Leibniz does not think finite beings possess any simple property, for he thinks all the simple properties are perfections possessed only by God. Perhaps it would be more accurate, therefore, to avoid speaking of creatures as possessing 'degrees of **P**', and speak only of 'degrees of approximation to **P**'. Let 'degrees of **P**', in what follows, be understood as an abbreviation of the latter, more accurate expression.

We may well be tempted by the following objection to this construction. It may work as a construction of the *relational* (and specifically, *comparative*) property of being one-billionth as powerful as a perfectly powerful being (provided there are no insuperable problems about a cardinal measure of degrees of power). But it may be thought that such a positive comparative property can only supervene on non-comparative properties which, if not simple, do have positive constituents that are not comparative and that the possessor of the comparative property must possess — whereas in the construction proposed above for Leibniz, there is no provision for a positive, non-comparative property to be possessed by the creature as part of the basis for its possessing the positive comparative property.

That's just the way it is with scalar magnitudes, a Leibnizian may reply; they don't have to supervene on non-comparative properties in the way that the objector claims. Some properties of finite things vary, primitively, in intensity or strength. Their variant forms just are degrees of scalar magnitudes of qualities that in their unqualified or absolute form are attributes of God. Just as it may seem that one light or shade of colour is brighter than another, and that this difference does not supervene on any more fundamental qualitative difference, so in fact a creature's degree of power, or of distinctness of perception, just is an inferior degree of the absolute power or knowledge that belongs to God — and the degree of the power or knowledge does not supervene on any more fundamental positive features of it.

This Leibnizian response is clarifying in a way. There are scalar magnitudes — for instance, length and velocity. It is not obvious that particular magnitudes within such a scale must supervene on any more fundamental feature of their possessor. But length and velocity are quantities rather than qualities in traditional Aristotelian terms; and for Leibniz, at least in his maturity, they are relational rather than directly qualitative features of things. There are properties normally and naturally counted as qualitative that we speak of as if they were scalar magnitudes in that way; (phenomenal) brightness is a good example of that. But I think it is far from obvious that anything can have a degree of (phenomenal) brightness that is not determined by positive qualities on which it supervenes, qualities which are not just degrees of a scalar magnitude.

That comparative degrees must supervene on non-comparative positive qualities is a point that I think applies to phenomenal qualities in general, and not just to brightness. I doubt that a particular shade of purplish red, for example, can be constructed as the property of being so many degrees (perhaps 217 thousandths) of the way from pure red to pure blue — even if there is a pure red and pure blue, and a cardinal measure of degrees along the spectrum between them, which may also be doubted. Knowing the pure red and the pure blue, and that the shade in question is 217 thousandths of the way from the former to the latter, will I be able to know what that shade of purplish red looks like? I think not. Knowing how it is related, by likeness and unlikeness, to other shades of colour is one thing; knowing what it looks like is another. And what it looks like *is* the shade of phenomenal colour. I think the project of constructing a particular phenomenal quality from relations of similarity or degree or partial negation to supposed 'pure' phenomenal qualities is probably doomed to failure because it involves substituting largely structural content for purely qualitative content, and the positive, purely qualitative content cannot be given in that way. And that may be a problem for comparative constructions of positive qualities in general.

Remarkably, Leibniz seems to embrace a somewhat similar conclusion on the basis of similar examples in one of his papers from 1676, saying

> There are infinitely many simple forms, because our perceptions are infinitely many and cannot be explained from each other, as from the knowledge of perception and extension alone it is impossible to explain what we sense in the red, the luminous, or the hot.[26]

In his maturity, however, Leibniz would not be concerned to refute what I have said about phenomenal qualities as such; for he regarded them as

[26] A VI, iii, 521.

complex rather than simple,[27] on the ground that they must be constituted by structures isomorphic with those of physical states that we perceive by means of them, though we are not normally conscious of this because our perceptions of them are confused. Leibniz's theory of universal harmony requires this mutual structural expression. So in his final view phenomenal qualities are less acceptable than knowledge and power as examples of relatively fundamental properties of things.

But a focus on knowledge and power hardly gives us a construction of positive properties of finite things as comparative properties that do not supervene on non-comparative properties. For it is not plausible to think of either the knowledge or the power possessed by a creature as just a degree of a scalar magnitude. It may *have* a degree of a scalar magnitude of knowledge or power; but that is just the point I have already granted to Leibniz, that a *comparative* property of degree of power (or knowledge) relative to the absolute divine power (or knowledge) may be constructible in the way I have suggested on his behalf. Comparative properties commonly supervene on non-comparative properties, however. And it seems that degrees of knowledge and power do supervene on facts — quite complex and not obviously comparative facts — about what their possessor knows and can do, and how.

Simple Qualities and Divine Perfections

The point just noted, about degrees of knowledge and power, and the complexity involved in them, connects with our remaining major question about the plausibility of identifying the simple qualities (if there are any) with the divine perfections. Doubts can arise about several points in the role that Leibniz assigns to the attributes of God. To what extent are they really *qualities*, as distinct from, say, relations? Don't such attributes as omniscience and omnipotence have a relational aspect, with regard to what is known and what can be brought about? And are

[27] In an important paper of 1686 (C 360) colours are among 'confused phenomena of the sense' that can be considered as '*primitive simple Terms*, or those to be assumed for them in the meantime', but in the context this pretty clearly means only that it is reasonable for us to leave them unanalysed, in scientific work, because the confusion of our perceptions leaves us unable to analyse them into anything simpler.

they *purely positive*? Doesn't omniscience involve negation, at least in the structure of its object, 'since even the imperfections or limitations of things are represented in the divine intellect', as Leibniz himself says? How plausible is it to suppose that an omniscient being can represent the negative just by representing the positive, as Leibniz seems to go on to suggest (Gr 355)? These questions deserve investigation, but here I want to focus on the question whether divine attributes, such as omniscience and omnipotence, are *simple*. For the top-down strategy of Leibniz's theory of the constitution of properties relies on a structure in which simple properties are the fundamental building blocks and are identified with divine perfections.

However, there is reason to doubt the simplicity of the divine perfections that are most salient for Leibniz and for theological and philosophical tradition. For example, *omniscience* does not seem to be simple. It seems rather to be analysable as knowing everything. If knowing is a simple property at all, it would seem to be a property indefinite as to the quantity of what is known. And omniscience (that is, knowing *everything*) seems to be a special case of it — a complex property constructed by further specification from the more general and simpler property of knowing as such. That construction is more plausible (at least on first reflection) than the one in which the property of knowing everything is identified with knowing as such, and properties of knowing less are constructed from it by limitation. And of course the literature of epistemology is rich in proposed analyses of knowing which suggest that it is not a simple property at all. Even if we are not satisfied with any complete conceptual analysis of it, we may think that knowledge must necessarily have complex structural and relational features that may lead us to doubt that it is thoroughly simple.

I do not think the mature Leibniz would insist on the simplicity of omniscience, or of perfect knowledge. As I have noted above, simplicity is not as essential as pure positiveness to his conception of a perfection. And by the beginning of his middle years he was denying that human analysis is capable of reaching concepts which are 'primitive' or 'conceived through themselves' (C 514). I take this to imply that we do not know that knowledge, in its divine form, or any other attribute that we conceive to be divine, is simple, since a simple attribute would be primitive and conceived through itself. Does this mean that Leibniz has no problem regarding the possible complexity of omniscience or perfect knowledge?

It does not imply, at any rate, that there is no problem here for his project of a top-down understanding of the properties of finite things as constructed from simple divine attributes. Let's consider two ways in which Leibniz might try to make that project compatible with his acknowledgement that we cannot identify any attribute as truly simple. I think we will find that each way may sustain a part of the project, but they do not together sustain quite the whole project.

First, so far as I can see, Leibniz never ceased to believe that all simple properties are properties of God. In the same text from which I have quoted the claim that our analysis cannot reach primitive or simple concepts, he says that God is the only thing of which a primitive concept can be a concept. It's just that 'we do not understand distinctly enough how the natures of things flow from God, nor how the ideas of things flow from the idea of God' (C 513). So why can't he continue to maintain that all the properties of finite things are in fact constructed from simple properties that belong to God and not to the finite things, even though we don't know how, nor from what properties?

The problem is that in ignorance of those things, we are given too little reason to believe that Leibniz's account of the construction is correct. Not knowing what the simple properties are, we have little reason to believe either that they are of transcendent perfection or that finite things do not possess them too. The following is one way in which simple properties might be possessed by finite beings, and not be of transcendent perfection, and yet all be in God. Finite substances, or monads, in Leibniz's final view of things are all perceiving substances; and in the last analysis there is nothing in them but perception and appetite (G II, 270/L 537), with perceptions as the sole occurrent qualities, and appetites as dispositions to perceive. If their properties are at least partly constructed from simple properties that they themselves possess, those will all be properties pertaining to perception — for instance, properties of having perceptions of a certain qualitative character. If God is a perceiving being, and omniscient, God may be presumed to have perceptions of every possible simple qualitative character, so as to understand perfectly all possibilities. And if that is so, other things Leibniz believes suggest that the eternal possibility of finite things having perceptions of those simple qualitative characters depends on God's necessarily and eternally having perceptions of those qualities.[28] Thus we may get the Leibnizian and Kantian thesis that all the positive qualitative content of all possible properties of creatures is found in God.

This is not a top-down account, however, because it does not explain properties of finite things in terms of *more perfect* properties of the infinite. In this account, rather, *the same* simple properties that are present in finite things are present also in God. This will still leave more than enough difference between God and the finite being to ground the numerical distinction between them as substances. For in God, we may suppose, there are vastly more of the simple properties than in any creature, and they occur in an immeasurably richer context. One by one, however, the simple properties themselves, which God shares with creatures, will hardly be of transcendent perfection.

The other line Leibniz might take may yield a top-down understanding of some, but not all, properties of finite things. It abandons the focus on simple qualities. We may therefore return to perfect knowledge as an example, without worrying now about whether it is simple. We may even return to the thought that it is not knowledge in general, without regard to its degree of perfection, but perfect knowledge that is the primitive case or form of knowledge. Only this will not now be grounded in claims about simplicity. Rather we will focus on ways in which human claims to knowledge are rendered unclear or uncertain by the imperfections of our cognitive condition. Intuitively, knowledge is supposed to be certain, justified, reliable, and produced in a non-defective way. Notoriously, however, the satisfaction of these requirements by any human cognition can be doubted. Many philosophers, perhaps most, insist none the less that we do know things; but our epistemological perplexities may lend some plausibility to the idea that what we call knowledge in our own case is only an approximation to a more perfect cognitive state that would fully be knowledge. They may even suggest the thought that we are not

---

[28] For reasoning tending to such a conclusion, see Robert M. Adams, 'God, Possibility, and Kant', in *Faith and Philosophy*, 17 (2000), 425–40.

in a position to understand what 'full-fledged' knowledge would be, but that one who had divinely perfect knowledge would understand it, and would understand better than we do in what ways we do and do not know.

An example may bring out the appeal of these thoughts. We ascribe beliefs and purposes to dogs. We do this by using as models beliefs and purposes that humans have, but that dogs could not have in the form in which they occur in the models. And surely we understand the dogs' thought better than we could if (*per impossibile*) we allowed in our minds only the sort of beliefs and purposes that dogs have. In this way we understand the dogs' thought better than dogs can. And we do it by using as a model our own more perfect consciousness — more perfect in the sense that it is more complete, including more complete instances of belief and purpose. Couldn't something similar be true of the relation of God's perfect knowledge to what counts as knowledge in us?

What is proposed here is a top-down account of the nature of knowledge, in which the perfect case is the primary case. The primary case is not omniscience as such. It may imply omniscience; but what is seen as archetypal in this line of thought is not how much God knows, but how God knows. And the primary case not only need not be simple, but is not viewed as a constituent from which less perfect cases are constructed, but rather as an archetype which they imperfectly resemble. The idea of a top-down account in which the key relationship is the more or less holistic one of resembling, rather than the more analytical one of being constructed out of, resonates with a long succession of texts of at least broadly Platonic origin, including some from medieval philosophical theologians.[29] Perhaps it is not unreasonable to see this idea also in section 48 of the *Monadology*, where Leibniz says that to the extent that they have perfection in them, attributes of created monads 'are nothing but imitations' of divine attributes.

This is, as I said, a top-down account only of *some* properties of finite

---

[29] For a particularly interesting example, see S. Bonaventura, *Commentaria in quatuor libros sententiarum Magistri Petri Lombardi*, lib. I, dist. 35, art. unicus, qu. 1, in his *Opera omnia*, ed. patres Collegii a S. Bonaventura, vol. I (Quaracchi: Typographia Collegii S. Bonaventurae, 1882), pp. 600–602; quoted, in part, in Marion, *La théologie blanche de Descartes*, p. 37. Marion's own comments about exemplarism in medieval and seventeenth-century philosophy are interesting (*ibid.*, pp. 37–50).

beings. The imperfect resemblance that our cognitive state may have to perfect or unqualified knowledge doubtless supervenes on other properties of our cognitive state; and nothing said here gives reason to deny that our state possesses those other properties precisely and completely. What gets a top-down account here is not how we possess any cognitive properties at all, but how those we possess may count as knowledge, albeit imperfect knowledge.

More generally, this sort of top-down account would be an account of *perfections*, explaining how finite things may be excellent or rich in some respect, in some degree, by their resemblance to the way in which an infinite being would be perfectly excellent or rich in that respect. Along these lines there might be top-down accounts of metaphysical perfections, such as substancehood, and of epistemological perfections, such as knowledge and understanding, as well as of moral and aesthetic perfections. None the less it remains plausible to suppose that the limited perfection of finite things always supervenes on other properties that cannot be constructed simply as incomplete or diminished likeness to transcendent perfections.

We could combine this line of thought with the other that I suggested for Leibniz, according to which simple properties from which a complete basis for all the properties of finite things may be constructed are also present in God, though they may not be transcendent perfections. The two lines of thought are compatible with each other. But the combination of them will not give Leibniz a top-down account of all properties, for the one is not a top-down account and the other does not apply to all properties, but only to perfections as such.

Note. Some of the material of this essay derives from the fourth of the Gifford Lectures on 'God and Being' that I gave at the University of St Andrews in November 1999, although that lecture had a less historical, more constructive focus.

7

Comments on Adams
'The Priority of the Perfect'

MARIA ROSA ANTOGNAZZA

IN HIS RICH AND INSIGHTFUL PAPER, Robert Adams has explored the priority of the perfect in the thought of Descartes, Spinoza and Leibniz, that is, their 'top-down' theories of the constitution of the properties of finite things in terms of their relation to the more perfect properties of the infinite. In doing so, he has devoted special attention to Leibniz's attempt to formulate a general top-down theory, identifying two Leibnizian strategies for explaining the properties of finite things in terms of their relation to the most perfect. The first of these strategies is a top-down account in which the key relationship between finite and infinite, imperfect and perfect being is the analytical one of 'being constructed out of' simple properties. In the second of these strategies the key relationship between finite and infinite, imperfect and perfect being, is the holistic one of resembling. Significantly, in this second case, the focus on simple qualities is abandoned.

I would like to highlight four points which in my view could help in unpacking the significance, importance and, at the same time, difficulty of the 'top-down' project pursued in philosophical theology by Descartes, Spinoza and Leibniz among others:

1 Top-down' versus 'bottom-up' explanation. What is to be gained?
2 Ontological and epistemological priority.
3 Why is a *general* 'top-down' theory of the constitution of the properties of things sought?
4 Simplicity.

Proceedings of the British Academy, **149**, 117–131. © The British Academy 2007.

'Top-down' versus 'bottom-up' explanation

Adams writes (p. 92): 'a "bottom-up" strategy . . . is appropriate and fruitful in many contexts. But I think it is well worth exploring the hypothesis that there are also important contexts in which a "top-down" strategy of understanding and representing the less perfect in terms of the more perfect or more complete will be the best.' In which sense and in which contexts would a 'top-down' strategy be best? What is to be gained in explanatory power that could not be gained from a 'bottom-up' strategy? The answer to these questions will help explain why such a 'top-down' project is so cherished by the Platonic tradition (and in particular, although not exclusively, by the various forms of Christian Platonism), and why it might be worth pursuing also today. Clearly, among the contexts in which the dichotomy 'top-down' versus 'bottom-up' takes place, one of the most important is philosophical theology. A 'top-down' strategy explains the relationship between God and finite things in terms of dependence of the latter on the former. More precisely, it does so by showing the dependence of the properties of finite things on those of God. Its gain is not only to show that God is the cause of finite things, but more specifically that God's properties are the ontological grounding of the properties of finite things. In other words, God is the root or ground of all reality, even of whatever degree of reality is in non-existing possible things. Could this result be gained from a 'bottom-up' approach of the kind defended by Gassendi and Locke according to which the idea of the Supreme Being is reached by 'enlarging' our idea of finite things? Even though a 'bottom-up' approach could yield important results in philosophical theology, it would not establish the ontological dependence of finite things from God. On the contrary, it is exposed to the suspicion of anthropologism: our idea of God could be a mere fiction, created in our own image and likeness.

Moreover, in a comparison of 'top-down' and 'bottom-up' approaches in philosophical theology, it is perhaps worth noting that a 'top-down' strategy strongly relies on the premise of the 'intelligibility' (non-contradictoriness) of experience. Although this is true also of other ways of reasoning in philosophical theology, the premise of the intelligibility of experience does not seem to be of such paramount importance for the success of a 'bottom-up' explanation of the most perfect (which lies beyond experience) in terms of the less perfect (which is within our experience). For the success of this strategy, it is enough that we are able to 'enlarge' the ideas of the things of which we have experience without the need to ask questions about the ultimate intelligibility of this experience.[1] This strategy, therefore, requires less but yields also significantly less. It does not aim at explaining our experience and does not ensure that our 'enlarged' idea of this experience corresponds somehow to some being. On the contrary, a 'top-down' strategy purports to account for both the intelligibility of experience and the existence of the Perfect Being the properties of which provide the ontological grounding of the properties of finite things. Finite things, in this view, would be unintelligible without the infinite; the less perfect would be unintelligible without the most perfect. Their intelligibility requires the postulation of this Infinite or Perfect Being which grounds our experience of the finite and of the imperfect but lies beyond it.

So there is a great deal to be gained from a 'top-down' approach in a (theistic) project of philosophical theology. But is it possible? In order to reflect on this question I would like to bring to the foreground a distinction that lies behind the thesis of the priority of the perfect shared by Descartes, Spinoza and Leibniz, namely the distinction between ontological priority and epistemological priority.

Ontological Priority and Epistemological Priority

With which kind of priority are we dealing when the priority of the perfect is affirmed? Are we dealing with the priority of the perfect *quoad se*, that is, its priority in itself, its ontological priority? Or are we also dealing with the priority of the perfect *quoad nos*, that is, its priority in the way in which we come to have some sort of idea of perfect and less per-

---

[1] As Adams shows in his paper, one could of course argue with Descartes that this very ability to 'enlarge' or 'amplify' ideas of limited perfections presupposes an idea of infinite perfection and is therefore itself an argument in favour of a top-down approach.

fect? It seems that Descartes affirms both kinds of priority straight away. This is particularly patent in the passage from the Third Meditation quoted by Adams (p. 91): it is from the ontological priority of the infinite, that is from the fact 'that there is more reality in infinite than in finite substance' that Descartes infers that 'the perception of the infinite is in some way prior in me to that of the finite'. In other words, Descartes moves from an affirmation of the ontological priority of the perfect to the affirmation of its epistemological priority as well. Now, this is famously a very debatable move, open as it is to the empiricist objection beautifully summarised by the quotation from Gassendi in Adams's paper (p. 95). Experience tells us that there is no epistemological priority of the perfect. Rather, we derive and construct an idea of the perfect 'of some sort for our own use' by denying the limitations that we find in our ideas of imperfect things. It seems to me that neither an ontological argument for the existence of God nor a top-down theory of the constitution of the properties of things can get off the ground before it has been shown that we can attain an idea of the perfect which is not itself just a 'bottom-up' construction from our ideas of imperfect beings. In other words, is there an epistemological priority of the perfect? Or, less strongly: even if there is not an epistemological priority of the perfect, is there a way in which we can plausibly reason about the ontological priority of the perfect deriving from it a top-down theory of the constitution of the properties of things?

It seems to me that this was the problem that Leibniz was addressing when he famously pointed out to the Cartesians that the ontological proof of the existence of God was incomplete. In order to complete it one needed to demonstrate the possibility of the idea of God on which the proof is based. This is the notion of *ens perfectissimum* or *ens realissimum*, that is, a notion of God that is not merely the Gassendian 'idea of some sort for our own use' but an idea of God that purports to grasp at least to a significant extent what God really is — *quoad se* and not merely *quoad nos*. It seems to me that any top-down theory of the constitution of the properties of things (including Leibniz's theory) also ultimately rests upon having satisfactorily shown the possibility of the *ens perfectissimum* or *ens realissimum*, and this in turn amounts at least to saying that even if there is not an epistemological priority of the perfect, we can somehow acknowledge its ontological priority and reason about it.

How then can the distinction between ontological priority and epistemological priority be bridged? In Descartes, Spinoza and Leibniz one undoubtedly finds a certain amount of 'sliding' from one priority to the other due to what could be called their shared 'rationalism', that is their conviction that our thought is able to 'track down' to some significant extent things as they really are.[2] One could even argue that it would be impossible to think without presupposing that thought has some grip on reality — the question being merely one of the degree or extent of this grip. This reality could for instance be only phenomenal, or the reality of nominal essences, but it would still be some degree of reality to which our thought relates. But even granting this, the issue at hand is whether our thought somehow 'tracks down' a specific kind of reality, namely the most rich in ontological reality of all: the *ens realissimum* or *ens perfectissimum*. Is the 'sliding' between the ontological and the epistemological priority justified in this specific case? To be sure, from God's perspective there is no gap between conceptual priorities and metaphysical priorities; and epistemological priority in relation to God's knowledge will be ontological priority for properties.[3] But this is *God's* perspective as opposed to ours. The question still remains of how this distinction can get bridged *quoad nos*.

One could reply by saying that even *quoad nos* the logical priority of the perfect is undeniable. But logical priority is a priority *ex hypothesi*: if there is a most perfect, it is logically prior to the less perfect. But is there a most perfect? Or, more precisely, can we be sure that the utterance 'most perfect' or *ens perfectissimum* corresponds to a possible concept in the sense that it does not entail a contradiction? We are back here to the problem (pointed out by Leibniz) of having first of all to prove the possibility of the notion of *ens perfectissimum* or *ens realissimum*.

---

[2] This was pointed out by Robert Adams in his response to a first version of these comments.

[3] Once again, this remark was part of Adams's response to the first version of these comments. Adams noted that this is one of the ways in which the distinction between ontological and epistemological priority gets bridged in Leibniz.

Now, this demonstration is a very ambitious project.[4] For present purposes, however, it is perhaps enough to focus on the weaker claim that
even if it is granted that there is no epistemological priority of the perfect
we can acknowledge its ontological priority and reason about it. I would
like to suggest two different ways (both running through the philosophical tradition) in which this claim could be supported: the first one
hinges on the thesis that in philosophy God is first found as a predicate
and not as a subject; the second one is based on the claim that we do
have an original, positive idea of the perfect, albeit very confused and
inadequate.

God as a Predicate

In *The Only Possible Argument in Support of a Demonstration of the
Existence of God* (1763) Kant noted that it is improper to say '"God is an
existent thing" . . . Strictly speaking, the matter ought to be formulated
like this: "Something existent is God". In other words, there belongs to
an existent thing those predicates which, taken together, we designate by
means of the expression "God".'[5] In other words, God in philosophy is
first found as a predicate and not as a subject because philosophy needs
to start from something that is immediately evident to everyone. It is not
immediately evident that we originally have a concept of God (that is,
that the word 'God' refers to a possible thing as opposed to being a mere
name — like the utterances 'square circle' or 'the fastest motion' — which
does not correspond to a concept).[6] Accordingly, philosophy can arrive at
the concept of God but cannot start from it. Before having successfully
argued for the existence of a being endowed with certain attributes, and

[4] Leibniz's proof of possibility is magisterially discussed in Adams, *Leibniz*, pp. 141–76.
[5] Section I, First Reflection, 2 (in Immanuel Kant, *Theoretical philosophy, 1755–1770*,
trans. and ed. David Walford, in collaboration with Ralf Meerbote (Cambridge:
Cambridge University Press, 1992), p. 120. For the following remarks I am indebted to
Sofia Vanni Rovighi, *La filosofia e il problema di Dio* (Milan: Vita e Pensiero, 1986), esp.
pp. 19–23.
[6] In the *Meditations on knowledge, truth, and ideas*, Leibniz discusses the example of 'the
fastest motion' (*motus celerrimus*) as something impossible of which we mistakenly pre-
sume to have an idea because we understand the single words that compose the notion in
question (G IV, 424; A VI, 4, 588–9). (For an explanation of references to the works of
Leibniz in this form, see Abbreviations, p. ix.)

which we indicate by the name 'God', we cannot be sure whether the name 'God' (or the utterance 'ens perfectissimum') corresponds to a true concept.

This is indeed the path followed by Anselm in the *Monologion*. The starting point is our experience of various things which we consider good. This experience is shown to require something that is supremely good and that, as such, is also the highest being and must have certain attributes. It is not until the last chapter that Anselm concludes that this is what is signified by the name 'God'. It is worth noting that this argument — reproposed by Thomas Aquinas's fourth way and found also in Augustine[7] — is clearly of Platonic origin and could be interpreted as an attempt at a top-down construction of the properties of limited things from the attributes of the highest being, such as supreme goodness. The less perfect goods that we find in our experience of different things, in order to be intelligible, ought to be understood in terms of the most perfect good. Interestingly, the argument quite explicitly keeps epistemological and ontological priority distinct. There is no epistemological priority of the perfect in that what is prior *quoad nos* is our experience of limited goods. From this experience it is however possible to arrive at the priority of the perfect *quoad se*, that is, at its ontological priority as the ontological grounding of whatever goodness we experience in finite things.

The path which does not start from God but finds God at the end as a predicate is consistently followed by Thomas Aquinas, who famously concludes what he regards as 'the first and more manifest way' to demonstrate the existence of God — namely the argument from our experience of change or becoming — with the assertion that the immutable Being at the existence of which the argument arrives 'is what everyone understands by God'.[8] Assuming that these *a posteriori* arguments for the existence of God are valid, while demonstrating the existence of God one has also reached a concept of God that can no longer be suspected of being mere *flatus vocis*. There is no epistemological priority of the

[7] Cf. Thomas Aquinas, *Summa Theologiae*, part I, q. 2, art. 3 and Augustine, *De Trinitate*, VIII, III, 4.
[8] *Summa Theologiae*, I, q. 2, art. 3.

perfect and of the infinite, in the sense that our perception of them is not prior to that of the finite; but the perfect and infinite can nevertheless be attained by our mind and its ontological priority acknowledged. Hence a top-down project that relies on the priority of the perfect is possible.

Our Idea of the Perfect

There could be, however, another way of acknowledging the ontological priority of the perfect bridging the distinction between ontological and epistemological priority. The fact that our understanding of the infinite is and cannot but be extremely deficient due to the limitation of our mind does not necessarily imply that our concept of the infinite is purely negative, namely that we represent the infinite 'only by negation of the finite',[9] and that therefore *quoad nos* there is no priority of the perfect. In his response to the 'First Objections' to the *Meditations*, Descartes both defends the positivity of our concept of the infinite (or, more precisely, of the 'thing which is infinite') and, at the same time, its extreme incompleteness (AT VII, 113–14; CSMK II, 81):

> I distinguish between the formal concept of the infinite, or 'infinity', and the thing which is infinite. In the case of infinity, even if we understand it to be positive in the highest degree, nevertheless our way of understanding it is negative, because it depends on our not noticing any limitation in the thing. But in the case of the thing itself which is infinite, although our understanding is positive, it is not adequate, that is to say, we do not have a complete grasp of everything in it that is capable of being understood. When we look at the sea, our vision does not encompass its entirety, nor do we measure out its enormous vastness; but we are still said to 'see' it. In fact if we look from a distance so that our vision almost covers the entire sea at one time, we see it only in a confused manner, just as we have a confused picture of a chiliagon when we take in all its sides at once . . . In the same way, God cannot be taken in by the human mind, and I admit this, along with all theologians. Moreover, God cannot be distinctly known by those who look from a distance as it were, and try to make their minds encompass his entirety all at once.

Following this path, the 'sliding' between ontological and episte-

[9] AT VII, 45. I follow here Adams's translation (p. 91).

mological priority seems to be justified after all. Our thought not only has some grip on reality but also 'tracks down' to some extent the specific kind of reality represented in the notion of 'most perfect', although in a very confused and inadequate manner.

Leibniz's theory of knowledge could provide further support for the claim that we have a positive but very confused and inadequate idea of the infinite thanks to his insistence on the different degrees of knowledge. Building on the difference (stressed by Descartes himself) between 'clear' and 'distinct',[10] Leibniz denies that certainty always demands clear *and* distinct ideas.[11] In his *Meditations on knowledge, truth, and ideas* (1684) he writes (G IV, 422–3; A VI, 4, 586–7):[12]

> Knowledge is *clear*, therefore, when I have that from which I can recognise the thing represented, and this [clear knowledge] is in turn either confused or distinct. It is *confused* when I cannot enumerate one by one the marks which are sufficient to distinguish the thing from others, although the thing really has those marks and requisites in which its notion can be resolved . . . Whereas a *distinct notion* is like the notion that assayers have of gold, namely [a notion established] through marks and examinations which are sufficient to distinguish the thing from all other bodies . . . But in composite notions, since sometimes the single component marks are in turn clearly but nevertheless confusedly known — such as heaviness, colour, aqua fortis, and others which enter into the marks of gold — such knowledge of gold although distinct is nevertheless *inadequate*. But when all that enters into a distinct notion is in turn known distinctly, that is when the analysis is carried through to the end, knowledge is *adequate*[.]

The snag is that in clear but confused knowledge could hide a contradiction, in which case the alleged knowledge would turn out to be no

---

[10] Cf. Descartes, *Principia Philosophiae* I, 45.

[11] Cf. *Réflexions sur la seconde réplique de Locke*, c. 1699–1700 (A VI, 6, 29): 'la certitude ne demande pas toujours des idées claires et distinctes. Je crois pourtant . . . que toute certitude demande quelque chose de clair dans les idées qui la font; et lorsque c'est une certitude de raisonnement et non pas seulement de sentiment je croy qu'il y faut encor quelque chose de distinct. Mais il n'est pas nécessaire que l'idée soit entièrement claire et distincte. Je fais différence icy entre clair et distinct, suivant l'usage des modernes et de Descartes même.'

[12] My translation. A complete translation of the *Meditations on knowledge, truth, and ideas* is included in L 291–5.

knowledge at all. Until the analysis has been conducted 'to the end' (*ad finem usque*) we cannot be absolutely certain that no contradiction will appear. Applied to the positive but confused and inadequate original idea that we have of the perfect, we cannot be certain that a contradiction is not lurking in it. So we are back to the problem of having to demonstrate beforehand either the possibility (that is, non-contradictoriness) of the notion of *ens perfectissimum*, or (without starting from the concept of God) the existence of a being endowed with certain properties and called God. As Leibniz put it in the *Meditations on knowledge, truth, and ideas* (G IV 424; A VI, 4, 588–9):[13]

> And certainly it happens that we often falsely believe ourselves to have in our mind ideas of things, when we falsely suppose that certain terms which we use have already been explained by us: it is not true or certainly is exposed to ambiguity, what some say: that we cannot speak of something and understand what we say without having an idea of it. For often we understand these single words in some fashion, or remember having understood them earlier, yet because we are content with this blind thinking and do not sufficiently pursue the resolution of notions, the contradiction which the composite notion may involve remains hidden to us. I was made to consider this point more distinctly some time ago by the argument for the Existence of God famous for a long time amongst the Scholastics and renewed by Descartes . . . it is not enough that we think about the *Ens perfectissimum* in order to assert that we have an idea of it, and in the demonstration referred to above the possibility of the *Ens perfectissimum* must be either shown or presupposed [*aut ostendenda aut supponenda est*] to reach a correct conclusion.

A General 'Top-Down' Theory

Assuming that it has been satisfactorily shown that the notion of *ens perfectissimum* is a true concept, why is a *general* 'top-down' theory of the constitution of the properties of things sought? Why should one not be satisfied with showing that a 'top-down' account can be provided at least for *some* properties of finite things? Both Descartes and Leibniz

[13] My translation.

might be seen as succeeding in this second, more limited, project. Descartes, for instance, proposes a conception of finite being which is constructed from that of infinite being (identified with being as such) by taking something away from it.[14] Leibniz, in turn, might take a line in which the perfect case is the primary case constituting an archetype which less perfect cases imperfectly resemble.[15] As outlined by Adams, however, the structure of Descartes's philosophy does not possess the resources for providing a general 'top-down' theory due to the Cartesian thesis that some of the limited perfections of finite things are not present in God formally, but only eminently. As for the (broadly Platonic) line which Leibniz might adopt of the imperfect resemblance to a perfect archetype, Adams argues that it 'may yield a top-down understanding of some, but not all, properties of finite things' (p. 114). This kind of top-down account would in fact be 'an account of *perfections*' (p. 116) and not, generally, of the properties of finite things which could still constitute the 'base' on which the limited perfections of finite things supervene.

The problem is that only a *general* theory can achieve the goal of showing that the perfect or the infinite provides the ontological grounding of all reality, of all the positiveness of finite things. If there are properties of finite things which are not explained in terms of dependence on the properties of the infinite, much of the interest and significance of this project of theistic philosophical theology seems to evaporate, notably its aim of providing the *last instance* of explanation for the intelligibility of our experience of finite things. There would be in fact properties of finite things that appear to be ontologically independent of the properties of the *ens perfectissimum*, such as Cartesian extension or the Leibnizian positive properties that could still be required as the 'base' on which limited perfections supervene.

Of the three authors discussed by Adams, it seems that Spinoza best succeeded in providing a general 'top-down' theory, but the price to be paid is that his all-reality-grounding God *is* all reality full stop. Although in itself a powerful theory, Spinoza's solution would never do for a 'top-

---

[14] See Adams's paper, p. 96. As Adams points out, however, the thesis that infinite being (or also infinite knowledge and infinite power) are being, knowledge and power as such, must be subjected to scrutiny to ascertain whether it is 'correct, or even plausible' (p. 98).
[15] See Adams's paper, p. 115.

down' theistic project of philosophical theology aiming at establishing transcendence and avoiding pantheism.

Simplicity

If what one is looking for is a general 'top-down' theory avoiding pantheism, neither Descartes nor Spinoza provide it. What about Leibniz? Of the two strategies which Leibniz could adopt — on the one hand, the construction of the positive qualities of the finite out of simple divine attributes; on the other hand, the holistic approach in which the key relationship between finite and infinite, imperfect and perfect being is that of resembling — it seems that only the first one might yield a general top-down theory. Can it be rescued?

'On this view' — presented by Adams as Leibniz's most articulated top-down conception — 'the less than perfect properties of finite things must all be composed, by logical operations including various degrees of limitation or partial negation, from the simple perfections of God' (p. 106). The pivotal concept here is that of 'simplicity'. Simple properties, identified with divine perfections, are the fundamental building blocks out of which the positive but less perfect qualities of finite things are constructed. Adams highlights the problems faced by this strategy. They derive from the very concept of *simple* property on which the theory is based. Taking as an example the perfection of power, he notes (p. 107): 'On a Leibnizian account the perfection of power should be partly denied and partly affirmed of finite things. But how can an absolutely *simple* property be partly denied of anything? What part of it is to be denied, and what part affirmed, given that it has no parts at all?' He then goes on to show — persuasively to my mind — that a comparative construction of positive qualities is probably doomed to failure because comparative degrees must supervene on non-comparative positive qualities.

One could wonder, however, whether the conception of simplicity adopted by Leibniz could not have in itself the resources to address the problem identified by Adams, namely the problem of how an absolutely simple property can be partly denied and partly affirmed of anything, given that it has no parts. Adams himself points out that Leibniz adopts an innovative conception of divine simplicity, consistent with his mature monadology, according to which a real plurality of distinct properties does not count as parts that could disturb the simplicity of a substance.[16] One might wonder whether this conception of simplicity could be brought to bear also upon the simplicity of attributes themselves. Granted that, from an ontological point of view, substances and attributes obviously belong to two different classes of entities, one might ask whether it would be possible to conceive of a simple attribute having different 'aspects' that do not disturb its simplicity, as in the case of the plurality to be found in simple substances. If this were possible, then, perhaps, an absolutely *simple* property would not be *partly* denied or affirmed of something (since it has no parts) but could be denied or affirmed of something according to one (or more) of its 'aspects'.

Now, according to Leibniz, substances are simple when they do not have parts that are or could be substances.[17] So only substances seem to qualify as possible 'parts' of a substance. This seems to provide a first argument against the possibility of bringing to bear the concept of simplicity that Leibniz applies to substances on another ontological class

[16] In this regard I would like to mention an early text in which Leibniz addresses the objection according to which the Trinitarian conception of God introduces a multiplicity that destroys God's 'most strict unity' and introduces imperfection (cf. A VI, 1, 526). Ontologically, the doctrine of the Trinity is clearly a harder case to reconcile with the doctrine of God's unity and simplicity than the presence of a plurality of really distinct attributes in God. However, basically consistent once again with his mature monadology, Leibniz replies (A VI, 1, 526–7): 'Non potest dici Deum ita strictissime unum esse, ut non dentur in eo realiter seu ante operationem mentis distincta . . . Neque hoc imperfectionem in Deo infert, quia multitudo et compositio per se imperfecta non est, nisi quatenus continet separabilitatem . . . Sed separabilitas hinc non infertur.' That is — adopting an almost Spinozistic conception of parthood according to which 'a thing composed of different parts must be such that each singular part can be conceived and understood without the others' (quoted by Adams, p. 99) — the persons of the Trinity are not 'parts' that could exist (not even intelligibly) without the others. Therefore they do not destroy the unity and simplicity of God (see *Remarques sur le livre d'un Antitrinitaire Anglois* (in Maria Rosa Antognazza, 'Inediti leibniziani sulle polemiche trinitarie', *Rivista di Filosofia neo-scolastica*, 83, 4 (1991), 549: 'les trois personnes ne sont pas des parties de l'unique substance divine absolue'. *A fortiori* a plurality of really distinct attributes does not disturb the simplicity of a substance.

[17] Cf. Adams's paper, p. 104.

of entities, namely attributes or properties. Obviously they could not have parts that are or could be substances, but it becomes trivial to say so since they are not substances in the first instance but what inhere in a substance and could not be without a substance in which to inhere. Still, one could explore whether there might be other ways in which the notion of simplicity in the case of properties could be developed to accommodate the hypothesis that simple properties, *qua* simple, do not have parts but might be denied or affirmed of something according to one (or more) of their 'aspects'.

This seems indeed to be possible in the conceptual framework of Spinoza's philosophy.[18] Finite modes of thought and of extension are incomplete expressions of the divine attributes of thought and of extension. One could perhaps interpret this incomplete 'expression' of the divine attributes by the finite modes as the expression of the divine attribute under some (and not all) of its 'aspects' without having to admit that the divine attribute has parts — where a part is intended (with Spinoza) as something that could at least intelligibly exist without the others.[19] Indeed, in Spinoza's system, finite modes are included under the appropriate attribute in the divine substance in the sense that they *are* the divine substance in one of its expressions. So, for instance, the divine attribute of thought could be expressed in the human mind according to some of its 'aspects' without being analysed into parts. Once again, however, the price to be paid is the denial of transcendence and the affirmation of pantheism — a price that Leibniz doubtless did not intend or want to pay.

Conclusion

As Adams has shown, the 'top-down' accounts of the three great early modern continental philosophers — Descartes, Spinoza and Leibniz — fail (for different reasons) to provide a general top-down theory that would

[18] The Spinozist outcome of this hypothesis was pointed out by Adams in his response to the first version of these comments.
[19] Cf. Spinoza, *Opera* I 24–5, (*Short Treatise*, I, ii). Referred to by Adams, p. 99.

satisfy the aims of a theistic project of philosophical theology wishing to avoid pantheism and affirming transcendence. On the other hand, the fact that the top-down approach seems to have gone out fashion due to the modern tendency to seek to understand (especially in scientific contexts) the more perfect and developed in terms of the less perfect and more rudimentary does not detract from its being well worth pursuing in appropriate contexts. The very persistence of top-down attempts at explanation in the history of philosophical theology from Plato onward bears testimony to the great promise held by such a strategy.

Bibliography

Note: For collected works of Descartes, Spinoza and Leibniz, see p. ix, 'Abbreviations'.

Adams, Robert Merrihew, 'God, Possibility, and Kant', *Faith and Philosophy*, 17 (2000), pp. 425–40.

Adams, Robert Merrihew, *Leibniz: Determinist, Theist, Idealist* (New York: Oxford University Press, 1994).

Adams, Robert Merrihew, 'Where Do Our Ideas Come From?—Descartes *vs.* Locke', in S. Stich, ed., *Innate Ideas*, pp. 71–87.

Allen, M. J. B., *The Platonism of Marsilio Ficino* (Berkeley, CA: University of California Press, 1989).

Antognazza, Maria Rosa, 'Inediti leibniziani sulle polemiche trinitarie', *Rivista di Filosophia neo-scolastica*, 83, 4 (1991), pp. 525–50.

Ariew, R. and J. Cottingham (eds.), *Descartes' Meditations: Background Source Materials* (Cambridge: Cambridge University Press, 1998).

Armstrong, A. H., *An Introduction to Ancient Philosophy* (London: Methuen, 1972; first published 1947).

Armstrong, A. H. and R. A. Markus, *Christian Faith and Greek Philosophy* (London: Darton, Longman and Todd, 1960).

Aubrey, John, *Brief Lives* [*c.* 1680], ed. O. Lawson Dick (Harmondsworth: Penguin, 1962).

Augustine, St, *De Trinitate*, in *Corpus Christianum, Series Latina* (Turnhout: Brepols, 2001), vol. 50.

Ayers, Michael, 'Ideas and Objective Being', in *The Cambridge History of Seventeenth-Century Philosophy*, ed. D. Garber and M. Ayers (Cambridge: Cambridge University Press, 1998), vol. II, pp. 1062–107.

Ayers, Michael, 'Theories of Knowledge and Belief', in *The Cambridge History of Seventeenth-Century Philosophy*, ed. D. Garber and M. Ayers (Cambridge: Cambridge University Press, 1998), vol. II, pp. 1003–61.

Ayers, Michael, 'Was Berkeley an Empiricist or a Rationalist?' in K. Winkler (ed.), *The Cambridge Companion to Berkeley* (Cambridge: Cambridge University Press, 2006), pp. 34–62.

Basil, St, *On the Holy Spirit* [*De spiritu sancto*, *c.* 370], ed. C. F. Johnston (Oxford: Clarendon Press, 1892).

Baumgarten, Alexander Gottlieb, *Metaphysica*, 7th edn. (Halle: Hemmerde, 1779; reprint Hildesheim: Georg Olms, 1963).

Proceedings of the British Academy, **149**, 133–137. © The British Academy 2007.

Betty, L. Stafford, 'The Anthropic Cosmological Argument', *International Philosophical Quarterly*, 27, 4, (1987), pp. 409–35, reprinted in M. Peterson *et al*. (eds.), *Philosophy of Religion: Selected Readings* (Oxford: Oxford University Press, 1996), pp. 198–210.

Bonaventura, *Commentaria in quatuor libros sententiarum Magistri Petri Lombardi*, in his *Opera omnia*, vol. I.

Bonaventura, *Opera omnia*, ed. patres Collegii a S. Bonaventura (Quaracchi: Typographia Collegii S. Bonaventurae, 1882–85).

Burnyeat, M. F. 'Plato', *Proceedings of the British Academy*, 111 (2001), pp. 1–22.

Coleridge, S. T. *Biographia Literaria* (Princeton, NJ: Bollingen, 1983).

Coleridge, S. T. *Collected Notes* IV (London: Routledge, 1990).

Colie, Rosalie, 'Spinoza in England, 1665–1730', *Proceedings of the American Philosophical Society*, 107 (1963).

Cornford, F. M., *Plato's Cosmology* (London: Routledge, 1937).

Cottingham, John (ed.), Descartes's *Conversation with Burman* [1648] (Oxford: Clarendon Press, 1976).

Cottingham, John (ed.), *The Cambridge Companion to Descartes* (Cambridge: Cambridge University Press, 1992).

Cottingham, John, *Philosophy and the Good Life* (Cambridge: Cambridge University Press, 1998).

Cottingham, John, '"The only sure sign . . ." Descartes on Thought and Language', in J. M. Preston (ed.), *Thought and Language* (Cambridge: Cambridge University Press, 1998), pp. 29–50.

Cottingham, John, 'Cartesian Dualism: Theology, Metaphysics and Science', in John Cottingham (ed.), *The Cambridge Companion to Descartes*, pp. 236–57.

Cottingham, John, 'The Cartesian legacy', *Proceedings of the Aristotelian Society*, Supp. vol. LXVI (1992), pp. 1–21.

Coudert, Alison P., *The Impact of the Kabbalah in the Seventeenth Century. The Life and Thought of Francis Mercury van Helmont (1614–1698)* (Leiden: Brill, 1999).

Craig, Edward, *The Mind of God and the Works of Man* (Oxford: Oxford University Press, 1987).

Cudworth, Ralph, *A Treatise Concerning Eternal and Immutable Morality*, ed. S. Hutton (Cambridge: Cambridge University Press, 1996).

Curley, Edwin, *Behind the Geometrical Method* (Princeton, NJ: Princeton University Press, 1988).

Donagan, Alan, 'Spinoza's Theology', in D. Garrett (ed.), *The Cambridge Companion to Spinoza* (Cambridge: Cambridge University Press 1995), pp. 343–82.

Eliot, T. S., *Collected Poems* (London: Faber and Faber, 1974).

Frede, Michael, 'An Empiricist View of Knowledge', in S. Everson (ed.), *Companions to Ancient Thought I: Epistemology* (Cambridge: Cambridge University Press, 1990), pp. 225–50.

Gabbey, Alan, '*Philosophia cartesiana triumphata*. Henry More (1646–1671)', in T. M. Lennon, J. M. Nichols and J. W. Davis (eds.), *Problems in Cartesianism* (Kingston and Montreal: McGill-Queens University Press, 1977), pp. 171–249.

Garrett, Don (ed.), *The Cambridge Companion to Spinoza* (Cambridge: Cambridge University Press, 1996).

Gaukroger, S., *Cartesian Logic* (Oxford: Clarendon Press, 1989).

Gilson, E., *La Philosophie de Saint Bonaventure* [1924], trans. I. Trethowan and F. J. Sheed (London: Sheed & Ward, 1938).

Goodman, L. E., 'Maimonides, Moses', *Routledge Encyclopaedia of Philosophy* (London: Routledge, 1998), vol. 6.

Greville, Robert, Lord Brooke, *The Nature of Truth: Its Union and Unity with the Soule, etc,* (London: Samuel Cartright, 1641).

Grua, Gaston, *Jurisprudence universelle et théodicée selon Leibniz* (Paris: Presses Universitaires de France, 1953).

Gueroult, Martial, *Spinoza*, vol. I: *Dieu (Éthique, I)* (Paris: Aubier-Montaigne, 1968).

Hankins, James, *Plato in the Italian Renaissance*, 2 vols. (Leiden: Brill, 1990).

Hutton, Sarah, 'The Prophetic Imagination. A Comparative Study of Spinoza and the Cambridge Platonist, John Smith', in *Spinoza's Political and Theological Thought*, ed. C. De Deugd (Amsterdam: North-Holland Publishing, 1984), pp. 73–81.

Joachim, H. H., *A Study of the* Ethics *of Spinoza* (Oxford: Oxford University Press, 1901).

Israel, Jonathan I., *Dutch Jewry in the Age of Mercantilism 1550–1750* (Oxford: Oxford University Press, 1985).

Israel, Jonathan I., *The Radical Enlightenment. Philosophy and the Making of Modernity* (Oxford: Oxford University Press, 2000).

Kant, Immanuel, *Theoretical Philosophy*, 1755–1770, trans. and ed. David Walford, in collaboration with Ralph Meerbote (Cambridge: Cambridge University Press, 1992).

Kaplan, Yosef, *From Christianity to Judaism. The Story of Isaac Orobio da Castro* (Oxford: Oxford University Press, 1989).

Kristeller, P. O., *Eight Philosophers of the Italian Renaissance* (Stanford, CA: Stanford University Press, 1964).

Leibniz, Gottfried Wilhelm, *Philosophical Essays*, ed. and trans. R. Ariew and D. Garber (Indianapolis, IN: Hackett, 1989).

Leibniz, Gottfried Wilhelm, *Theodicy*. English translation by E. M. Huggard (London: Routledge & Kegan Paul, 1951).

Lennon, Thomas, *The Battle of the Gods and the Giants: The Legacies of Descartes and Gassendi* (Princeton, NJ: Princeton University Press, 1993).

Locke, John, *An Essay Concerning Human Understanding*, ed. Peter H. Nidditch (Oxford: Clarendon Press, 1975).

Locke, John, *The Correspondence of John Locke*, ed. E. S. de Beer, 8 vols. (Oxford: Oxford University Press, 1976–89).

Long, A. A. and D. N. Sedley (eds.), *The Hellenistic Philosophers* (Cambridge: Cambridge University Press, 1987).

Méchoulan, Henri, *Amsterdam au temps de Spinoza* (Paris: Presses Universitaires de France, 1990).

Menn, Stephen, *Descartes and Augustine* (Cambridge: Cambridge University Press, 1998).

Montaigne, Michel, *Les essais de Michel, seigneur de Montaigne* (Paris, 1657).

More, Henry, *Philosophical Works* (London, 1712).

More, Henry, *A Platonick Song of the Soul*, ed. A. Jacob (Lewisburg, PA: Bucknell, 1998).

Nadler, Stephen, *Spinoza. A Life* (Cambridge: Cambridge University Press, 1999).

Nussbaum, Martha, *The Fragility of Goodness* (Cambridge: Cambridge University Press, 1986).

Oderberg, D. S., 'On the Cardinality of the Cardinal Virtues', *International Journal of Philosophical Studies*, 7, 3 (1999), pp. 305–22.

Parkinson, G. H. R., *Spinoza's Theory of Knowledge* (Oxford: Oxford University Press, 1954).

Pascal, Blaise, *Pensées* [*c.* 1660], ed L. Lafuma (Paris: Seuil, 1962).

Plotinus, *Enneads*, in *Plotinus with an English Translation*, trans. A. H. Armstrong, 7 vols., 2nd edn (Cambridge MA: Harvard University Press, 1988, first published 1966).

Popkin, Richard H., 'Christian Jews and Jewish Christians in the Seventeenth Century', in R. H. Popkin and G. M. Weiner (eds.), *Jewish Christians and Christian Jews* (Dordrecht: Kluwer, 1994).

Popkin, Richard H., *Spinoza* (Oxford: One World Publications, 2004).

Rodis-Lewis, G., *Descartes* (Paris: Calmann-Levy, 1995).

Rogers, G. A. J., 'Locke and Platonism' (forthcoming).

Ross, Donald L., 'Plotinus the first Cartesian?' *Hermathena*, 169 (2000), pp. 153–67.

Roth, Leon, *Spinoza* (London: E. Benn, 1929).

Rorty, Richard, *Philosophy and the Mirror of Nature* (Oxford: Blackwell, 1980).

Rutherford, Donald, *Leibniz and the Rational Order of Nature* (Cambridge: Cambridge University Press, 1995).

Schmitt, C. B. and Q. Skinner (eds.), *The Cambridge History of Renaissance Philosophy* (Cambridge: Cambridge University Press, 1988).

Scholem, Gersholm, 'Die Wachtersche Kontroverse über den Spinozismus und ihre Folgen', in K. Gründer and W. Schmitt-Biggemann (eds.), *Spinoza in der Frühzeit seiner religiosen Wirkung* (Heidelberg: Schneider, 1984), pp. 15–25.

Schufreider, G., *Confessions of a Rational Mystic* (West Lafayette, IN: Purdue University Press, 1944).

Smith, John, *Select Discourses* (London, 1660).

Spinoza, B. de, *The Collected Works of Spinoza*, trans. Edwin Curley (Princeton, NJ: Princeton University Press, 1985).

Spinoza, B. de, *Benedicti de Spinoza opera quotquot reperta sunt*, ed. J. van Vloten and J. P. N. Land, 4 vols. (The Hague: Martinus Nijhoff, 1914).

Spinoza, Benedict, *Renati des Cartes principiorum philosophiae . . . (etc)* (Amsterdam, 1646).

Taylor, A. E., *Does God Exist?* (London: Collins, 1966).

Thomas Aquinas, St, *Summa Theologiae*, Blackfriars edn. (New York: Blackfriars and McGraw-Hill Book Co.; London: Eyre and Spottiswoode, 1963–80).

van Bunge, Wiep, *From Stevin to Spinoza: an essay on philosophy in the seventeenth-century Dutch Republic* (Leiden: Brill 2001).

Vanni Rovighi, Sophia, *La filosophia e il problema di Dio* (Milan: Vita e Pensiero, 1986).

Wilson, Catherine, 'The Strange Hybridity of Spinoza's Ethics', in C. Mercer and E. O'Neill (eds.), *Early Modern Philosophy: Mind, Matter and Metaphysics* (Oxford: Oxford University Press, 2006), pp. 86–102.

Wilson, Catherine, 'Soul, Body, and World: Plato's *Timaeus* and its Reception in Early Modern Philosphy', in S. Hutton and D. Hedley (eds.), *Platonism at the Origins of Modernity* (Dordrecht: Springer, 2007), pp. 177–91.

Wilson, Margaret, 'Spinoza's Theory of Knowledge', in *The Cambridge Companion to Spinoza*, ed. Don Garrett (Cambridge: Cambridge University Press, 1996).

Wolfson, Harry Austryn, *The Philosophy of Spinoza: Unfolding the Latent Processes of his Reasoning* (Cambridge, MA: Harvard University Press, 1934).

Index

on our idea of the infinite 91, 124
  see also being; perfection
on our idea of God 10, 13, 62, 91–8
and monism 62–3
as moderniser 17, 32, 37f, 41, 92
and contemplation 29–32, 48–9
Pascal on 20, 60
Spinoza on 55
design, intelligent 21–2, 24, 25n
Donagan, Alan 102n

Einstein, Albert 50
Eliot, T. S. 49n
empiricism
  significance of the term 1–3
  and the New Philosophy 1–2
  and materialism 4
  and science 47
  see also Spinoza, materialism of; Spinoza,
    and empiricism
ens perfectissimum, realissimum 92, 104–5,
  120–1, 126
  see also perfection; being
Epicurus 3
Epistle of James 44n
eternal truths *see* Descartes, on eternal truths
Euclid 50
extension
  in Descartes 11, 68–9, 96–98
  in Leibniz 11, 102
  in Spinoza 11, 64–5, 67–9, 99–102

facies totius universi 66–7, 79
faith
  as highest form of cognition 59–60, 71
Ficino, Marsilio 29n, 45, 51, 81
finite things *see* being; creation; God; perfection;
Frede, Michael 2

Gabbey, Alan 82n
Galilei, Galileo 58
Gandhi 50
Garber, Daniel 2n, 72n,
Garrett, Don 85n
Gassendi
  as empiricist 2, 3, 57

on idea of God 93, 95, 120
Gaukroger, S. 26n
Genesis 20, 57–8
geometry 2, 14, 15, 56, 86
Gilson, Etienne 35
God
  idea of 10–11, 31–2, 66–7, 93–5, 118, 120
  as source of idea of perfection 29, 32
  as source of all being 29,
  as the Good 33, 43,
  as the One 62–3, 79,
  attributes of 11–12, 93–116
  corporeality or incorporeality of 69–70, 96–8
  imperishability and immutability of 59, 93
  mind, intellect of 26, 46, 48, 57, 65–7, 80,
    86–7 see also archetype, will
  omnipotence of 93, 111
  omnipresence and sempiternity of 93
  omniscience of 93–4, 111–15 cf. 100
  simplicity of 93, 98, 104–5
  emanation of universe from 7, 54, 60, 62–3,
    64–8, 79
    see also creation
  as craftsman 34n
    see also demiurge
  illumination by 11, 18–19, 29–33, 43–4, 58n,
    59–60
  causal argument for the existence of 95
  ontological argument for the existence of 48,
    105, 120–2
  purposes of 26
gravity 21–2
Greville, Robert, Lord Brooke 71
Grua, Gaston 104n
Gründer, K. 83n, 85n
Gueroult, Martial 100

Hankins, James 81n
Hegel, G. W. F. 48, 50
Heidegger, Martin 48
Herrera, Abraham Cohen 84
Hobbes, Thomas
  on necessity of laws 2, 73–4
  and Descartes 15
  and Spinoza 7–9, 56, 69–70, 73–4, 76, 85–6,
    89
  as object of attack 51, 69–70
Hume, David 26, 47
Hyperaspistes 94

Index